John Fuchs

FORTY YEARS AFTER GURDJIEFF

A GUIDE TO PRACTICAL WORK

Edited by Demian Smith

Published by
Gurdjieff Group of Denver
P.O Box 18849, Denver, CO 80218

Forty Years After Gurdjieff

A Guide to Practical Work

by John Fuchs

Published by
Gurdjieff Group of Denver
P.O. Box 18849, Denver, CO 80218

Publisher's Cataloging in Publication Data
Fuchs, John
Forty Years After Gurdjieff : A Guide to Practical Work / by John Fuchs.—
1. Spiritual life. 2. Gurdjieff, George Ivanovitch. I.Title

ISBN: 0-9641069-7-3 (Hardcover)
ISBN: 0-9641069-5-7 (Softcover)
Library of Congress Catalog Card Number: 94-76275

This book is dedicated to
John Pentland, Cynthia Pearce, and
Mme. Jeanne de Salzmann.

There is no book that is a substitute for the work that is transmitted by your teachers and the work that you do on yourself. For every idea there is a time and a level. Sometimes "you try" but at other times you do nothing but observe.

CONTENTS

I am most grateful to
DEMIAN SMITH,
whose help was invaluable to me.

Preface—A New Beginning

I was an ardent horseman. I remember the first hunter[*] I bought in the early forties. I loved it, and I was quite convinced that I was an excellent rider. One day a light went on in my head. I saw myself as I was and realized that, while I was athletic and could sit on a horse, I knew nothing about real horsemanship at all.

This I realized long before I knew what self-observation and self-remembering were. I had not met the Work yet and knew nothing about different centers, but I *saw* something. So I asked who was the best riding teacher on Long Island, where I lived, and was directed to a Swiss cavalry officer, Captain Vogt. Captain Vogt was the typical martinet. Picture a straight-backed gentleman, white mustache, black Derby, black riding coat, shiny black boots, a no-nonsense man.

Captain Vogt looked me over, looked over my horse and said, "Mr. Fuchs, I will take you on provided you keep quiet, listen to me, and only ask a question when I am through explaining." Cocky as I was, I had a choice of getting off the horse and punching Captain Vogt in the nose or saying, "aye, aye, sir," and submitting to authority. I recognized that to become a horseman instead of a "rider," I had to submit to authority, superior knowledge, learn obedience, and acquire a new kind of discipline.

Captain Vogt was thorough, scientific. He taught my mind all about horsemanship. I say "mind" because much later, through the Work, I learned that my moving center should have been educated and utilized, instead of the mind using the moving center to set the horse for a jump and to judge speed and distance.

I survived this tough school and joined the Oaks Hunt, a prestigious fox hunt on Long Island, participating joyfully in many

---

* The technical term for a jumping horse.

1

rough and taxing events. Through this, I cultivated self-recognition, honest self-appraisal, discipline, and submission. These were preparations for the Work, which I encountered years later.

Another kind of preparation came years before this period. I lived in Vienna at that time and as a college student spent every summer in the Alps. For four weeks, my friend "Bully" and I were above 14,000 feet on the glaciers with no professional guide. Bully deserved his name. He had thick blond hair, the bluest of eyes under black eyebrows, and he was built like a bull. With enormous self-confidence, mentally and physically, we were "self-sufficient," tied together by a rope, equipped with crampons, ice axes and heavy rucksacks.

Glacier work is something special, different from regular mountain climbing. You must sense, feel if the new snow will hold you or if it disguises a crevasse with a drop of a thousand feet into blue-green nothingness. What I am saying is this: we had to be totally present with every single step, to be "attuned" to something, a warning bell inside of us. Daydreaming (sleep) could mean a serious accident or even death.

In these ways, I learned that I could be present to myself and my surroundings at every moment. I acquired an awareness and a subconscious recognition that there is "something" which can guide us, help us, provided we are *awake*.

I am convinced now that these experiences were a preparation for what I was to encounter later. These lessons were a great help to me in the Work. They have shown me, over the years, that I must augment dry words acquired in meetings and books with vital, real experiences. Today, in my groups, I try to go beyond the written word and connect my students with personal life experiences such as the two I have described.

If there is any magic in words, their constant mechanical use destroys it. Our understanding is not merely the spoken words we hear but consists of our internal recognition of their *meaning.* In life, all words are taken as absolute. If they are taken absolutely, they are at best limited and at worst actually mislead us about what the Work intends to convey to us. And so I use words wrought out of my experiences to give you a sense, that glacier sense, of how to live the Gurdjieff Work in a very practical way.

Introduction

I have been asked why I want to write a book. I feel that forty years in the Work with teachers who have studied under Mr. Gurdjieff have given me a wealth of material and experiences. My teachers were among the last of the direct students of Mr. Gurdjieff and I was compelled to record their impact on my life.

I came into the Gurdjieff Work through what Mr. Gurdjieff called the magnetic center. I was groping subconsciously for something, something I knew existed but which was beyond my grasp. And so I began to read indiscriminately: Dion Fortune, Gina Cerminara, the *History of Magic* by Eliphas Levi. I did not learn magic. H.P. Blavatsky's books, *The Secret Doctrine* and *Isis Unveiled*, intrigued me. I was always seeking the mysterious, the unknown. Then I encountered Kenneth Walker's books, *So Great a Mystery* and *A Study of Gurdjieff's Teaching*. Dr. Walker alluded to study groups and teachers. Did these exist? Were they accessible to me? Thus, my magnetic center began to awaken.

All the groups mentioned were in Europe: London, Paris, and, prior to this, Moscow and St. Petersburg. I wrote to the publishers of Walker's books in London asking if Dr. Walker was still alive and if there were any teachers and groups in the United States. To my surprise, an answer came from Dr. Walker himself, telling me that there were indeed groups and teachers in New York City, where I lived, and I should see Lord John Pentland, who was then the head of all Gurdjieff groups in the United States. This was the beginning of my work.

After being interviewed by Lord Pentland, I was given the privilege of entering his study-group. Several months later, he asked me to join Cynthia Pearce, who was just forming a new group. Mrs. Pearce was an intimate friend of Madame de Salzmann who was the head of all Gurdjieff groups world-wide. In time Mrs. Pearce designated me the treasurer of the group, and later her assistant.

Mme. de Salzmann came to New York every year, from October to December and again from January to March. With her came Henri Tracol, her assistant in Paris. Group meetings were every Monday and sittings every Friday. I sat religiously five feet in front of Mme. de Salzmann to absorb her vibrations as directly as possible.

Thomas Forman, an assistant to Mrs. Pearce in meetings, and I had many a stimulating conversation and controversy. Sometimes Christopher Fremantle, the husband of the poet Mary Fremantle, took over when Mrs. Pearce was visiting her children and grandchildren in London, Johannesburg, or China. All of these, my teachers, had studied at the Chateau du Prieure under Mr. Gurdjieff.

Summers were devoted to work weekends at the country place of the Gurdjieff Foundation in Armonk, New York. These were intense periods, valuable and sometimes amusing, even at my expense. I remember this episode: I drove Mrs. Pearce to Armonk, where we met with our group and her Philadelphia pupils. The Philadelphians, the "guests," were quartered in a comfortable new house built by the New York people. We were billeted in an old barn with torn window screens, an invitation for clouds of mosquitos which kept us up half the night. The other half of the night I was kept awake by my own anxiety. I was given the task (with another man) of preparing breakfast down at the new house, to be ready and served at 8 A.M. after a "sitting" at 7. The menu was to be cooked cereal. Prior to this, my total cooking experience had been pouring cornflakes out of a box and making toast.

I was up at 5 A.M., down to the house at 6 to concoct breakfast. When it was served, Mrs. Pearce, in her inimitable aristocratic way, asked, "John, is this for eating or cement for the patio?" My colleague, having the task the following morning,

5

fared no better. His menu was "western omelette." Mr. Forman looked up and asked, "Is this omelette for eating or riding?"

This was the way friction was created, efforts were made. I was taught as my teachers were taught by Mr. Gurdjieff. This, in turn, is what I have tried to imbue in my own students since moving to Denver, Colorado, where I formed my own groups under Lord Pentland's tutelage and guidance. Until his death, he divided his time between San Francisco and New York. We maintained constant contact by phone, mail, and travel to San Francisco.

I have used the material my teachers gave me practically and profitably for myself in my daily life. I believe that I must pass on these experiences, made possible by my teachers and by my own efforts, to students of Gurdjieff who want a *practical* approach to their own immediate problems and questions, rather than a theoretical or philosophical one. Here you may find useful directions and help in facing the agonizing questions which touch each of our lives.

Chapter 1

Inner Transformation

Several years ago, there was a man in my group who started out bewildered, unsure of himself, groping for a direction in life. He was confused, torn. Recognizing this and seeing many of his weaknesses, he was determined to do something about his situation. Thus he entered the Work.

He attended meetings, sittings, made himself useful to me, the group, and the Work in every respect. He practiced self-observation as he went about his daily life more than anyone I have encountered in all the years I have been in the Work. His confidence grew and he set before him two goals: to become "a man" and to become "a man of the world." To be "a man" is to work on essence, seeking strength, fortitude, will, objectivity and total balance. To be "a man of the world" is to work on personality, seeking adaptability, understanding of life relationships, polish, tact, and being able to play the correct role in every life situation.

At most meetings he spoke up and described how he used the Work in his profession, his emotional life, always combatting his weaknesses. He took directions, often reluctantly and resentfully, but always recognizing their value and their help in becoming a different person. He started reading, which was not natural to him. Quickly, it became clear to him what a tool reading could be, not only to increase *knowledge*, but also *being*, by doing things which were against his former self. Thus he created friction.

Gradually he acquired discipline—first outer, then, slowly, inner. Gradually, he became firmer internally, making tougher decisions—tough on himself. He began to transform himself.

Can you recall your state before you found the Work? I experienced an inner dissatisfaction, a vague feeling that there existed something higher than what I had discovered "in life." This vagueness took form as the beginning of a search. A search for what? I didn't know; I couldn't define it. However, eventually help came from "something" which began to form in me, during my search through books, lectures, and study of esoteric literature, and brought me to this work.

Slowly, I began to understand what was required—an inner transformation. A real aim came into my life, a greater realization of what I was then and what I wished to become. I also saw that I needed help. Help toward inner transformation is available from groups and teachers and through actually working. You start each day with the "sitting," the morning exercise, in which quieting the body and mind is the first step toward self-remembering. You try to use the ideas and to do the exercises given. You attend group meetings, readings and work weekends.

As you go on, you see more and more that work on yourself must come from within. You must *do* the work; your teacher cannot do it for you, nor can the group. Gurdjieff said, "The Institute can only create the conditions; you have to do the work yourself." A group leader can only point the direction and explain what steps may be needed.

There are two approaches toward inner transformation that are very helpful. One is "total immobility." The other is "the wish." Total immobility can be both physical and mental. You straighten your spine, with the head balanced on the neck and shoulders, sensing your whole body and emptying your mind. In being "immobile," the possibility exists for a new internal state to arise in which I am empty but can be filled. I must remember that one reason I came to this work was to make room for something new. The glass that is already full cannot be filled with anything new unless it is first emptied. The state of total immobility enables us to "allow something to happen."

The state created by immobility comes from a very small, quiet place in me and, little by little, spreads out into my whole organism, producing the possibility of change, transformation. Still, I may notice a shallowness. My morning sitting has to take on a different quality. I need to be more quiet. Then I feel something growing in me. What seems to grow is the ability to face myself for a moment longer. Is this the beginning of what has been called the second Being Body?

The *wish* is the strongest force in the world for inner transformation. This force begins to act in me. The first thing in the morning, before my shower, before my coffee, before getting dressed, I make the commitment as I sit down: "I wish to be totally quiet today. I wish to tune into my higher centers, to enlist the help of my emotional center and through this make contact with higher forces." I direct my attention toward sensing every part of my body. I observe the functioning of the mind, still it, empty it, relax it and make it blank. I observe my breathing, but without interfering with it. When I have difficulties with all this, I continue trying to come back again and again to myself as I am, and, if a certain quiet is reached, I then attempt one of the many exercises given for self-remembering.

I have been speaking all along about *myself,* or rather the single individual. Somehow I feel, deep down in my heart, that this is incomplete. I feel that a group can experience the same transformation as the individual, only multiplied by the number of members of the group. I mean *members*, and not just passive participants. I use the word members because I feel a unity among the group; the group is a unit. I recall a meeting which had the solemnity of a church, though not the oppressive heaviness. After a long silence, a strange sentence came out, "We are more than a group at this moment, we are a brotherhood."

How can inner transformation be achieved? Mme. de Salzmann answered in her kind, inimitable way: **"You try."**

Chapter 2

Energy

Being an outdoor man, a man from the Austrian Alps, I look toward the mountains, "from whence cometh my help." When I am in need I get into my car and drive to a canyon 20 miles from my home. I park, put on my hiking boots, start walking, and open myself to the familiar, higher influences: the strength emanating from the rocks, the sweet fragrance of the pines—the sun and the blue sky. An inner transformation takes place, an inflow of higher energies, and when I return home I find something different in myself.

In my daily life when I look at my "doing the Work," when I see my attempts, I come to the realization that I need more energy for doing what I want to do. I also see my wish to prevent the leakage of the energy I have.

I can begin to stop leaking energy by struggling against my mechanical habits, by self-study, by self-remembering. A definite, limited quantity of energy is given us, produced by nature during our rest at night. This energy is sufficient to see us through the day, but it is limited and it is squandered on ordinary life so that nothing is left for inner work and development.

Can I plan how I want to expend my energy in my daily life and how much I will need for my inner work? I have to be watchful, observing myself all the time. One slip, one expression of negative emotion—if I get angry, violent—and I use energies which will take days, weeks to replenish. But the work is to transform these emotions of anger, fear or boredom. I need to be more present to these types of emotions so that they take on a different taste and begin to be useful to me.

10

In realizing this, I come to two conclusions. First, I am giving unnecessary energy to everyday activities. Second, I am leaking energy continuously by the expression of negative emotions, impatience, outbursts of anger, daydreaming, and internal considering. These may not necessarily be verbalized or voiced. They can take place internally and are equally detrimental and draining.

Internal considering is one of the most debilitating leaks of energy. Perhaps I feel I am not valued enough by others. I am identified with my feelings and thoughts about how people treat me and their attitudes toward me. I am misunderstood, people are not polite and courteous enough, I feel I am not respected. All this, of course, is my imagination. Yet it torments me and drains me of energy. It makes me suspicious of others, hostile, vengeful. Life is unjust, and so is the attitude of others toward me. I am continuously making accounts. I expect people to express esteem and admiration for me, recognize my cleverness, intellect, ingenuity, good taste, eloquence, and sophistication, and all around superiority. But I must try to see how devastating these attitudes can be. They can corrode my entire life and my relationships with people. As I try, I will see which of these aspects are attributable to me and make it my task to be especially attentive and observe them.

When I see that I am disillusioned with my life, I recognize what "dis-illusionment" is: it is the destruction of illusion. This is a beneficial state, because I realize that life the way I live it is an illusion. I begin to see reality, I step away from my subjective manner of thinking, and approach—for moments—objectivity. For moments I may be able "to do."

Another of the chief reasons that we leak energy is involuntary tension. I have to try to see myself, my body, reacting to circumstances. My fists are clenched in anger or determination. My jaws are tightly clamped. My shoulder muscles are tensed. I don't know why, but I sense my tension in my solar plexus and in my calf muscles. I even notice the curling of my toes. I say "notice." I should, but do I?

I made an observation one evening, sitting in my den. I saw myself putting both hands over my face and saying silently, "I am tired." I could feel the tension in my body. My whole attitude reflected this tension. Then I "woke up" and realized, "This is self-indulgence." Becoming aware of this, I looked at my attitude from the Work point of view: same chair, same gesture, but instead of saying "I am tired," which just made me more tired, I said, "I am resting now." By not being negative and draining myself with self-pity, I opened up to an influx of a new kind of energy and altered my state. How often do our physical tensions rob us of our energy?

So what do I do? I make observing myself my daily task, dividing myself into two, the observer and the observed. If I can *see*, if I have a strong enough attention, I can steer the mind away from a destructive trend of thought into positive directions, diverting the emotional center from a negative momentum and channeling it into a positive direction.

I become aware of the process of observation and see that it starts with sensing the entire body. This creates a space between the emotional reaction and the conscious presence and allows me to act instead of react. Observing myself, I begin to see my weakness when I indulge in negative emotions, expressing anger, internal considering, justifying. In time I may be able to catch my negativities at the right moment—before they are in control, before the momentum takes over and the car careens downhill without brakes.

One of the students in my group became quite upset when I said she was neurotic. But what does "neurotic" mean? It simply means the inappropriate substitution of one center for another or the wrong use of centers. This explanation not only calmed her but opened her to seeing herself in an entirely new way and discovering that many upsetting situations in life were due to using the emotional center with its high vibrations where cool intellectual evaluation would save enormous amounts of energy.

Self-observation can help me to see how much unnecessary physical energy I exert in my daily life. Perhaps when I pick up a pencil I do it as if it were a ten-pound weight. Or when cutting bread I use the force of my entire arm when only the pressure from my hand is required. My observations teach me to be economical and efficient in all tasks, and in time remind me to try those tasks consciously, not mechanically.

How much energy do I waste in a manual task performed or guided mainly by the moving part of the moving center, when the thinking part would have shown how much faster and more efficiently the task could be performed? Sit down, plan the job, lay out the tools in the sequence you will use them. Consider how to arrange the work so you won't have to walk back and forth constantly, and then let the moving center take over. The energy we save can be used in another moment for our inner work.

Practicing self-observation, I can acquire a surplus of energy at the end of the day—the energy required for inner development and the transformation which is our goal, our aim, and our birthright.

In addition to stopping the leakage of my energy, I can work to create more energy by increasing my own efforts.

If you had an upsetting day at work or at home, thoughts churning, mixed with emotions (anger, violence, self-blame, self-pity, apprehension about the next day), although energies are drained by all this, remember, not all energies are depleted. What is most likely expended is the emotional and intellectual centers' store of energy. Remember the third source is in the moving center. Put on your running shoes, jog a few blocks, get on your bike, go for a walk, have a workout. Not only is there enough physical energy left, but by using it in the above manner, you recharge the depleted batteries of the other centers—and above all you will be making a Work effort.

There are other ways. Music can make contact with your emotional center; a crossword puzzle or a paperback mystery can help make contact with the intellectual center. Make a phone call to someone who can stimulate any of those centers, even write in your journal. If you use these tools consciously, any of them will relieve the pressure of the present situation. These things, consciously done, will be of help to you. If done mechanically, they will be of no help whatsoever to your inner transformation.

This is self-awareness, attempting to live more consciously. I recall being asked by my teacher, very pointedly,

"John, do you practice living consciously every day?"

Your energy can also be increased by endeavoring to achieve internal immobility. When I do my morning exercise, I realize that the quality of my sitting corresponds to the quality of my energy. When I begin to enter the void, feel disembodied, approach the no-mind level, I try to hold this, prolong it. Still it fades away, escapes me. I know that if I had more energy, a different kind of energy, I could remain in this state for a longer time and possibly make contact with higher forces. This effort at creating and prolonging inner immobility, inner quiet, itself creates energy with finer vibrations. This is the law. Little by little this energy and these vibrations revert back to my body. They have a chemical, nay, an alchemical effect on my entire organism.

Here are four ideas which were of help to me with my question about energy:

1) I can conserve energy by thinking more consciously.

2) To prevent leaking of energy in depression, I have to make *efforts.*

3) I must have *lighter* thoughts and longer thoughts.

4) Inner quiet creates finer energy.

14

Chapter 3

Work on Yourself

The ordinary person must work on him- or herself daily if the possibility is to exist for that person to become conscious, to become a transformed being. By observing myself, I can see over and over again that I am in my ordinary mechanical state. How then do I begin? First I have to recognize the need to work on myself. This is a precondition and a work in and of itself.

To see, really see, how incomplete I am as I am, how I drift from one direction to another, brings the recognition that I need to work on myself. This very important condition for starting my work requires seriousness, honesty and strong desire.

In contact with the real aim, I make a commitment to pursue it. I don't permit myself to make excuses. It takes will and determination to cross the interval when confronted with, "I just don't feel like working now." Wishing is not enough. Unless I move, the process toward the higher will not continue. The level will stay the same or descend.

My own work starts with the morning exercise. It is in this exercise that you make your commitment to work on yourself *now*. Let this be your leitmotif during the day. As you move in life, learn to use the tools appropriate for your mood and/or external state. There are many that are at your disposal. There are exercises that can be used to awaken your commitment, your determination, your aim. If they are not connected to these, they will be of very little use. For example you can try taking mental pictures of yourself as you observe yourself. These photographs are observations that take in the whole of you, not just details, not only postures and physical attitudes, but the tone of voice, sensations, moods, emotions and thoughts.

Another exercise is to make a date with yourself to be completely, quietly aware of yourself, sense your body, remember yourself—say, at 10:30 in the morning and 4:30 in the afternoon. You may also listen to the sound of your voice. Where does it come from—from your head, your throat or from your innermost being? What effect does it have on the listener? These are "alarm clocks" which are designed to help you to remember yourself, to be aware of your being, and to get in touch with the Work. They will teach you to establish "the pause," the space, the vacuum which can enable you to think for a moment, to try to *act* when normally you would only *react*.

Other exercises that have been given to us to be practiced during the week range from the sensing of a coffee cup in your hand, to being aware of irritation, negativity, impatience or anger. It takes attention, and a special kind of energy to do these exercises as you try to "live the Work." I make it an aim to be present to my hands holding the steering wheel of my car. Other times I may try to eliminate my daydreaming from one stop light to the next. Your whole day gives you countless opportunities for physical, psychological and intellectual work on yourself.

You can create your own alarm clocks, your own aims and methods for being quiet, sensing your body. This is the means by which you implement in your life what you have been taught in the Work. It is necessary to be constantly changing and "recycling" the types of alarms after a certain time, since they become mechanical after a certain number of uses. I have also used the following successfully: For a certain period I try to be present when I look in the mirror and shave. Another time I try to be present when I lock the door upon leaving my house. I try to be present when I start the car.

Different work arises in difficult life situations. Perhaps I encounter anger in a person who is raising his voice at me. If I lower the pitch of my voice, this often moves the angry person to calm down. Doing this, I have saved and perhaps created energy as well as resolving an unpleasant situation. Suppose I have a luncheon date for 12:30 P.M. and the person does not show up on time, nor at 12:40, nor at 12:50 nor at 1:00 P.M. I have the choice to either become impatient, nervous, continuously looking at my watch, tapping my fingers on the table, or to make an effort to use the Work—trying not to react, sitting calmly, relaxed and working, accepting the situation. Accepting any situation that I cannot change is using the Work. This is a crossroads—I have the choice.

I have made some work efforts and the day is over—but is it? This is when a new level of effort can take place. At this point I can take a "work" book and study it consciously for twenty minutes. I make notes of the work experiences I had during the day in a journal. I record the "flashes" that perhaps explain some facet of my personality, or moments of enlightenment, or when I remembered to use a work tool that had been given to me. If I feel elated, I enter it in my journal. I record moments when I have seen my sleep. I note times during the day when I saw my resistance to the Work. It is as important and valuable that you see your wish *not* to work as your wish to work. My journals have been of great help to me in vividly seeing my growth or the lack of it. If a similar situation arises, I have a record of what I have already done. My journals give me a concrete way of comparing then and now.

Before going to bed, review the whole day, in as minute detail as you can. You will see how often you were asleep, how many gaps there are in your memory. You cannot even remember the proper sequence of events. Did the alarm clocks work? Were you negative? Did you lose force because of your negativity? The review of your day may take the form of pictures or words, depending on which center is speaking. Making this review, a subtle process begins to take place. You forget your tiredness. A new energy emerges in you. Your mind is refreshed and starts functioning. You feel you want "to do"—that is, to work on yourself.

Finally, I end my day as I began it. I go through a similar procedure to that of the morning exercise, going around my body consciously as an observer, relaxing every part of it. I try in my last moments before I sleep to be entirely in this moment, **here and now.**

Chapter 4

Payment and Sacrifice

Some years ago I was in Monument Valley, Arizona. It was evening in the desert. The "monument" stood silhouetted purple against the flaming yellow sky. A Navajo woman guided her sheep down the sand dunes and an indescribable peace entered my being. I felt an overwhelming gratitude for being here—for being and living. How can I ever pay for experiencing this moment? How can I pay for the gifts I have received in my life? What is the price of transformation?

When a person wishes to grow, a *payment* has to be made for advancing in his or her evolution and inner expansion. This is the law. We get nothing for free.

How do we pay? First, if we want something, we must pay with efforts—or, better yet, super-efforts. Effort needs knowledge and recognition of the moment when the effort is useful. Such efforts include doing a task well, being present to yourself as often as you can during your waking hours, seeing yourself attempting to be quiet and immobile when emotions are taxing your energies, sensing yourself and working to prevent your attention from being pulled out of you and absorbed in a life situation—that is, identifying. You engage in "intentional suffering" when you sacrifice your internal considering. Intentional suffering is payment; for example, when you refrain from expressing a negative emotion, this is a payment, as Mr. Ouspensky repeatedly mentions in *In Search of the Miraculous*. We would love to vent our ire, criticize a person or situation, or simply gossip or bad-mouth someone. Not doing it is intentional suffering. We all have experienced how hard this is, especially when we are personally attacked. It is at this time that we need to remember internal considering and if we can remember, this is payment.

Time is payment. We are allotted only a limited time in our life for our inner transformation. The time we give to the Work is payment. The remainder of the time is just life.

At one time my teacher asked me, "What have you sacrificed?" The question hit the mark and still makes me squirm. It is easy enough to enumerate small sacrifices, but when I look for the biggest one, it is *my time*. Nothing has created more inner conflicts since I endeavored living the Work than giving up my leisure time for the Work. Going to movements, sittings, work periods, and readings prevented me from doing many things I enjoyed doing in "life." I gave up Sundays to work with our group, painting apartments, cleaning houses, tending yards and lawns in order to raise money for the groups.

Giving time was the most difficult payment for me. I enjoyed horseback riding on weekends and had to sacrifice it. I sacrificed business trips not to miss a meeting or a sitting at the Foundation. Perhaps your sacrifice will be different. You may face family problems, being often away from home. It may be hard for you to let go of your own self-importance when you listen to your teacher.

Another manner of payment is your work for the group. Prepare your questions for the meeting by deep, sincere inner search, so that they come from your being and not from your mind. You can help the group financially. You attend meetings, movements, work weekends, readings, sacrificing your comforts and pleasures, often having to overcome obstacles in family and social life. Voluntary suffering is the greatest payment of all.

By the efforts I make, I demonstrate my valuation of the Work. These efforts embrace sacrifices in many forms, including sacrificing my pride, my vanity, and the lofty image I may have of myself. When I see how I fall short or when I recognize the quality—or the lack of quality—I give to my efforts, I am shown my weaknesses. My efforts show me who and what I am, if I am there to *see*. And this is a painful payment. It brings me to the point of asking myself, *What is my aim?* Without payment, I may eventually lose what I have learned and acquired in the Work.

Payment is a very important principle in the Work; this must be understood. You have to make payment before receiving anything and the first real payment is to take the trouble to study and understand the things you hear and read. This, in turn, creates the possibility, the conditions, required for the next levels of payment. You sacrifice imagination to live in the *real* world. If you work long enough, perhaps you will sacrifice your negativity, your anger, your laziness and your multitude of contradictory "I's." You may eventually be able to sacrifice who you are for what you can be.

I sit in my den surrounded by my books. Two Navajo rugs, dear to me, hang on the walls facing me. It is after dinner, after a hike, after doing the dishes. I want to relax, read a book, rest for a while. But the inner alarm bell rings and reminds me to work. I think of the commitment I have made to do some writing every evening. The alarm clock whispers, "This is the Work; this intentional suffering." The whisper becomes a loud clear ring—*sacrifice*. And so I sit down instead of reading an entertaining book which supports sleep, and, in payment for my transformation, I start writing.

Chapter 5

Help, Wish, and Prayer

I pondered on the efficacy of prayer. Or did I really ponder? It was more a daydream, and so I let my thoughts come in and pass through my mind until they revolved around a focal point, a conversation I had with my teacher Mrs. Pearce, who herself was a pupil of Gurdjieff in France. My thoughts slowly solidified and took me back into childhood. Mrs. Pearce had said, "As a child you were taught to pray, 'Please, God, bless Mommy and Daddy.' Later, you began to ask for things for yourself, a subtle change in the direction of the prayer. Such prayer can be addressed to an angel. You asked, 'Please help me find my toy.' Probably you found it."

But is this real prayer? Once one has attained responsible age, real prayer is very difficult to formulate, because it is difficult to recognize the levels involved. For how can a power which is *pure Love* be expected to hear a voice that just "wants" or "would like" something?

Wish is the ultimate expression of prayer. The Work tells us it is the most powerful force in the world. Through *wish*, vibrations are created which increase the function of our centers to their highest efficiency. But first, let us be clear, "I wish" is not "I want." In our usual state, wants come only from personality, from the part that either likes or dislikes, the part that is filled with duality and contradictions. "It" wants one thing one minute and something else the next. Wish is on a much higher level—I would almost say on a cosmic level on which higher forces work of which we have no concept. Planetary forces influence our lives. These are forces our magnetic center can attract and transform. They can act on essence. Mr. Gurdjieff tells us that even the Absolute will reach our essence at times. A real wish originates in our essence.

I have now connected wish with esoteric forces. How does the wish manifest itself in our planetary mind? What can I do on my part? I feel the mind, which "makes" us understand these forces, is at the same time the transformer of these same forces. We cannot voluntarily influence essence, but we are able to influence and use our mind if the wish is strong enough, if we have enough will and determination to pursue the aim, the wish. However, in our ordinary state, we are unable to maintain the intensity. We lose it and regain it again, maybe in a different form. We may not even recall how the wish originally was formulated and expressed, but we have a taste of it that remains with us.

You must try to see yourself objectively and sincerely before you find your wish. When do I ask for *help*? First, I must differentiate whether my wish is trivial. I have to ask myself, "Am I entitled to ask for help? Have I done all I could?" Am I sincere in asking, with my whole being, or is there a part in me which still feels, "I can handle this situation myself, with just a little effort?" Or if I wish, for example, for a better job, an advancement in position, when deep down in my heart I feel I am not ready for it and I fear its actualization? How can this kind of wish or prayer be answered when its realization would be to my disadvantage?

A prayer or wish can be made, however, regarding any kind of need. It can be in our daily life, a health problem, a family situation, children. It can be a job, difficulties with management, employer or fellow employees, conflicts with neighbors. We are identified *with* situations. We are identified *in* situations. We are submerged, unable to assess objectively, and we need help.

My prayer, my wish, must come from a deep inner need, from a humility which normally is alien to me. It is the motive in asking that counts. If my prayer is granted, it appears to be a miracle to me. But a "miracle" is only the manifestation of higher forces coming down from a different, higher plane which operates under different and fewer laws. This is the explanation of miracles. What we term a miracle is a natural occurrence according to higher laws, on a higher plane. Christ knew and must have lived under these laws when he performed his "miracles."

Who in you wishes? Who prays? From where does it come? Are you able to ask with complete attention, never losing the feeling of yourself for one second, being really aware of every word as you speak or shout it out loud? Can you feel your voice coming from and reverberating in your whole being, so that no part of you refuses to participate? You must make your prayer, your wish, your "God." It must be a matter of life and death for you. We must try to understand the meaning of this. Only if it comes from your entire being can it touch the source which will answer it. And the answer will be understood in accordance with the level of your being. At the point my being is ready to receive my wish, my prayer, it may arrive. The higher your state, the more you will understand the help given to you. Help can be received, if you ask humbly and sincerely. Mrs. Pearce said to me, "Do this with your whole heart. I have never experienced this to fail."

I have to put all of these questions in front of me—not in front of my mind, but in front of all of me. Then I can be truthful to myself, and objective enough to see if I deserve to ask the higher powers to show me the way. I do not know the way, my mind does not know it, book knowledge cannot give it to me.

Here are examples of the right kind of prayer: "I wish to see myself as I am." "I pray for understanding, for the ability to accept (not just endure); for being able to hear, to see." They are aspects of the objective love I so rarely can experience, since I am far from this high state of being. I need to look into this. The sentence "God help me" is a real prayer.

Realizing all of this, it is clear that the work of evolution requires a terrible integrity. "For I, thy God, am a jealous God; thou shalt have no other gods before me." Can this be taken absolutely literally? Who is this jealous God for me? It is the Work. Real prayer is a cosmic substance if properly produced. It is *material*, as everything in the cosmos is material. Thoughts, feelings, emotions are all material. Humans in their ordinary state do not possess this possibility of powerful prayer or real wish, since in their state of sleep prayer is useless and ineffective. Such prayer cannot be answered by any means other than by accident.

I was once told, "Say your prayers out loud, have them reverberating through your whole being. Ask with every part of you, and each time you ask you must ask the higher powers three times. Repeat it day after day. The answer will then come, not in your time, but in God's time. It may come in a totally unexpected form, and you must have the inner sensitivity to hear and see it."

Remember, you have to go on even when you think you are not heard. Help *is* available. If we ask for help, we instinctively look *up*, implying that the forces enter from above. But I must also turn *inward*. Two higher centers, the higher emotional and higher mental, are inside of us. We are born with them. They are in us from birth, working 24 hours a day, always ready, only we are not in contact with them. They can be reached through your emotional center. My task therefore is to develop, to refine this center. Then the higher centers can guide me.

God is inside of us, and the help we ask for may be in us already. The two higher centers which are there are completely developed, but working with much finer vibrations. There is help that can be reached through the higher emotional center that comes from the inner circle of humanity and guides the lives of three-brained beings in their present condition.

Help also comes from your work group. The questions asked

by others and the answers given often contain what you need for your own question or for your own problem. The different points of view enlighten you, widen your horizon. You feel you are not alone, your predicament or problem is not unique. The energies gathered from the years that you have been with a group can cause the group to act as the accumulator for you, supplying the support you need for your transformation.

You must practice to be able to pray, to make a sincere wish. You must persist in asking, perhaps even demand what you ask for. There is an active and a passive way to ask for help. The approach taken by some esoteric schools is to *demand* help. In this case your own will, your own wish, is the active force. You will have to choose which way to go. Perhaps, if you ask for something quite specific, such as help with a health problem, a demand combined with faith and belief can produce what we have called a "miracle."

If, on the other hand, you ask for understanding or enlightenment, you must be *passive*, and

allow something to happen.

Whichever approach we take, the forces that are within (as well as those outside of us) can give us help. But as I have said, it is in their time, not always when we want and expect it.

Finally, there is help possible from His Endlessness, from the Absolute, from God. All these influences are trying to help, but as long as I am identified with my suffering, false personality, buffers, anger, making accounts, self-pity, or memories of the past, these influences are unable to reach me, cannot free me and contribute to the expanding growth of my understanding.

So I turn to the Work. I turn it over to the Work. I am quiet, quiet and I wait. I, for myself, must feel it will come. I have heard and believe the words, "The Work is fifty times as strong as you are," and, "You *can* get help." These words become part of me, penetrating my organism and my life.

26

I usually say my prayers in the sitting position of my morning exercise, but sometimes I have the overwhelming urge to prostrate myself on the floor. I seem to sense my nothingness in those moments. I am aware of the forces radiating from above. Humbly I prepare myself to meet them.

Chapter 6

Loneliness

Why are we lonely—what brings it on, and above all, what can we do about it? How does it manifest itself? How can I come to grips with it? It is not solely an emotional state; all three centers of us participate in it:

Moving center,

Emotional center,

Intellectual center.

I notice a different sensation in the region of my solar plexus. My posture shows it, a collapse in my spine. I droop, my head hangs down, my step loses it's spring. I shuffle, slow down my pace. The corners of my mouth are turned down. My eyes are lusterless.

Now this is interesting: What comes first—is loneliness expressed in those physical symptoms—or do they produce my loneliness? Both: sometimes my loneliness starts in the moving center and produces the state I am describing. Sometimes it is reversed. The inner hollow loneliness finds expression in my physical state and posture.

Why? Many things. A thought can produce it—a memory of what I had or lost or of what I wished for. A melody going through my mind may open floodgates of experiences wished for or lost. A fragrance, a flower, perfume, a breeze in the air can turn on a whole chorus of different, usually negative, sad emotions.

Color, form can influence me. The flaming orange, pink and purple of a sunset can do it. A bright star on the firmament at night, the constellation of Orion, Cassiopeia, the Dipper, the Moon will influence my emotional center and again either bring back memories of the past or longing for something that lies in the unknown, in the future.

Last but not least, people. I can be terribly lonely in a whole group of people. At a cocktail party, at a concert—where music contributes an additional element to my loneliness. In the office, when I see people absorbed and identified with what they are doing. I can be lonely in talking to just one person, noticing the complete lack of mutual understanding, seeing in him or her the person asleep or self-absorbed, far removed from me, while we sit three feet apart.

And, of course, the opposite: not a person around—here I am, all alone—feeling sorry for myself.

Now comes the second part: what can I do about it? Gurdjieff tells us making an effort—an effort of any kind—can alter our inner state. It can be physical. Take a walk (and observe your breathing), go jogging, or turn to your favorite sport—tennis, skiing, horseback riding, volleyball—or just your usual gym exercises. Pick up a book from your library; your magnetic center may just lead you to the right kind of book for your mood.

Turn to music. You may play the piano or listen to a recording, find a program on your television, where again by accident or a miracle you push the right button.

Do you paint? Are you a sculptor? Do you like gardening or are you a gourmet cook? There are innumerable things you could do; make an effort. Do you meditate? Can you connect yourself with the real you, or something even higher—way above you—through an inner silence which transforms you, creates finer, higher vibrations in you, which produce this transformation?

All this can be done, can be of help to alleviate your loneliness. But it presupposes one thing: You must know yourself—

or try to know yourself. Know your functioning: physical, material, and psychic. Your self-knowledge may give you the key to your loneliness, may enable to see yourself as you are at this moment, this stage, in this state, and this may show you the direction your efforts should take.

Chapter 7

Sleep and Consciousness

It was dusk. I was walking in one of the narrow streets of Flo-
rence. As I passed the rows of 500-year-old wooden doors and
the wrought iron ornamental entrances to palaces that I had
never seen before I had the very real feeling: "I know this
place"—a feeling of *déjà vu*. This thought filled me with sensation; I felt it physically. Instantly I was completely aware of
my surroundings. I was *there*. This did not taste of sleep or
imagination or daydreaming. I started then to ponder what sleep
and consciousness really means.

The words "sleep" and "consciousness" have meanings
which go much deeper than what we read into them. We must
not take them literally as we use them in daily conversation, but
take them in their psychological meaning. They are designed to
be understood at deeper levels than what we understand from
ordinary life.What is the work meaning of these words? Mr.
Gurdjieff says that man is asleep. All our actions are in sleep;
they are mechanical. Our thinking, planning, functioning in
daily life is in sleep. We cannot act in sleep; we only react.

Sleep has different stages. Our sleep at night is valuable
physically and psychologically. Nature creates the energies we
require for the coming day. As we approach the point of "getting up," our body becomes restless, fidgety. Thoughts, or half-
thoughts enter as half-dreams. Slowly the thoughts take on
more substance and form, but we are still in the cocoon of sleep
until we finally begin to face the day.

Now we enter a different sleep, the sleep of mechanical man.
We react to everything and anything. We talk in automatic
phrases to express automatic feelings spun out by automatically

generated thoughts linked repetitiously by clustered associations. The wrong centers take over. Emotions just occur; the mind does not discriminate, spewing out thoughts. Our attention wanders, jumping from place to place, topic to topic. We are not present, not conscious. We do not focus our mind, our intellectual center but operate out of what Ouspensky calls the formatory apparatus, which takes over our thinking mechanically. We identify with every situation and allow imagination to dominate all the parts of ourselves. Gurdjieff refers to this state, seemingly in jest, as "clear consciousness" or "waking consciousness" although it is a state of being that is neither clear nor conscious.

"Waking sleep" is my ordinary state and it is from this state that I *must* escape if I want a change in my life. My life would be different if I could become conscious. Consciousness should be my life's aim. How do I go about pursuing it? I begin with AIM, with the commitment to strive for that aim constantly. I put this in front of me as I wake up, as I start the day: "I must observe, see myself, my sleep, and the sleep of the other people around me." This already wakes me up for a moment.

I get glimpses of myself. I am driving downtown to work. What goes on inside of me during this drive? Am I totally unconscious? Am I daydreaming? Do I get impatient at the length of the red light? Do I swear at the people that cut in front of me or are going too slowly, blocking me? This is sleep. But this morning I decided to observe myself; at one moment in my drive I see all this and I become conscious, aware of my hands on the steering wheel, aware of my surroundings as well as of what went on in me seconds ago. Yes, this is consciousness. Granted, it is fleeting, something that I cannot hold, but it is the first step toward being awake more often during the day.

For moments I sense myself, I see my posture, perhaps even hear my own voice, and then I fall asleep again. But, as it was my aim, I will again become the observer and will have moments of awakening. Gradually those times will become more frequent, longer, and the periods of sleep between them shorter. I visualize the day as being like a string of pearls. The pearls are in a heap in front of me. They are my waking moments, moments of consciousness. One by one I pick them up, when I have the sensation of myself, when I engage in "right thinking," when I control the mechanical expression of my feelings and recognize impatience, anger, curiosity, negativity, all within me. I string my pearls together patiently, making efforts of awareness, and maybe—at the end of the day, the week, the month—I have created a necklace of "being."

Chapter 8

Self-Remembering

I lived in those days on the north shore of Long Island, and boarded my horse in a nearby stable owned by the Gormleys, an old established Irish horse family of three generations. Old Hugh Gormley had taken a liking to me, and when I asked him if he would go out with me one afternoon and give me a few pointers on jumping fences he readily agreed. We went through the woods and came to the fences around Grace's East Field.

Hugh Gormley had given me a 17-hand powerful grey named Roger. We approached the fences and Roger sailed over them and then took off like lightning. I tried to rein him in—in vain. He had literally taken off. There was no holding back—no reining in. No power on earth could conquer him, and there I was—what to do? He was going too fast to jump off and too fast to stay on.

As we were galloping over the field I was strangely detached. I saw my self and my predicament. It was clear thinking—aware of what can or will happen, and still being "present," conscious, in a clear state of "self-remembering," as clear as sitting on my soft zafu in the morning exercise.

After a time I pulled. I sawed on Roger's mouth, determined to gain some sort of control. I saw the U-shaped mansion of the Whitney Estate—and my safety. Roger allowed me to rein him in. I steered Roger into the square and only then realized that I had been saved by a miracle. He stopped and for a time I did not dismount. I stayed with myself and the horse and the moment.

Behind me I heard the clippety-clop of horse's hooves and there was Mr. Gormley with a grin on his face, commenting drily, "Well, you stayed on."

Why do I go to the grocery store and forget everything I need? Why do I wake up in the middle of the night with a "very important" idea—which has evaporated in the morning upon waking up? Why don't I remember situations and events in the past which were outstanding events when they happened? The answer is: I was not conscious, I was not in "the state of self-remembering"—the state in which I do remember.

Self-remembering is a force. It is "material," as everything else is material—feelings, emotions, thoughts, even a view, a fragrance, or a melody.

The *act* of remembering myself precedes *the state of self-remembering*. The attempt to come to self-remembering has its origin for the searcher in the inner need to live on a different plateau.

This attempt to remember myself can be practiced in many ways, from sitting quietly, passively relaxing the body and mind and becoming aware of the breath gently moving the chest, to active self-observation during waking hours. There are exercises that appear, at first, unimportant and easy, but are in fact very difficult to perform.

To name just a few exercises I had given to the groups to practice: make an effort to remember yourself when you look in the bathroom mirror while shaving or at your dresser making up your face. Attempt to remember yourself sitting down at the breakfast table, both legs on the floor to "make contact"—feeling the warmth of your coffee or tea cup and enjoying consciously what you eat—being aware that this is the first being food. Become aware of the sensations—the smell and taste which are of the third being food, impressions.

Try to remember yourself when you handle your car keys. When you pick them up, on your dresser, in your pocket, in your handbag. When you start the car and when stopping you pull them out. Stay with it for a few moments. When you see that you do not remember yourself, feel remorse; this too can lead to self-remembering.

As I work in the group, as I sit with others in the group or as I speak, I can begin my attempts to remember myself. Outside the group there are the memories I can use of hundreds of hours of group meetings, lectures, intensive work weekends. There are the admonishments to establish inner quiet, create higher, finer substances. There is the wish to contact our higher centers, to create a higher being body, crystallize it. All these efforts are designed to lead one to the state of self-remembering.

Invent "alarm clocks" for self-remembering. Use them daily—but also change them before they become useless habits. Be also aware of one great trap: you may be convinced, "now I am remembering myself"—while instead you are identified with the exercise you have been practicing. Self-remembering is separating yourself from the "self," creating a space, a vacuum, for really seeing yourself. It should be in front of you, the monkey on your back, for all your waking hours.

But you must avoid deceiving yourself: I believe it is my mind, my intellectual center, which is self-remembering, and I think I have accomplished it. Yet self-remembering is not accomplished through the mind. Our mind is not us—it is only a small part of us. The mind has only one language which does not convince the other two centers—the emotional and moving centers.

This is just like the analogy in which the coachman's language does not communicate with the horse and the carriage. But it is only by the cooperation of those that the true state of self-remembering is created. Only the vibrations, the energies, the elements, of all three centers will produce self-remembering. Otherwise it is only a thought, a mental image, which makes you believe it.

No, the entire Being has to be involved, has to be transformed in those moments. Often something does not "taste" quite right.

Am I really remembering myself? Am I establishing the quality of consciousness I strive for? There is a faint doubt and a sense of imperfection. Am I missing something? Am I sincere? Have I made an inner connection? Do I really know what inner listening is—for me? Am I making a place within myself where the help which I need can enter and remain?

These questions bring about an awareness of what "objective consciousness" could mean. They can make me see the illusions I have about myself. The strange thing is that this is not destructive nor discouraging. On the contrary, it clears the air, brings in different vibrations which enable and force me to get a sharper image of what I am. They are the light that is consciousness and provide me with a hint of the direction which my inner work has to take.

I say hint, because only if the Work has made you sensitive enough, taught you inner listening, can you sense and feel what the next step has to be. Then you may be able to come into contact with your higher centers, where something else can take over.

I am in the mountains on my weekly walk. I think of being asked in the group: "Where is 'The Way?' Am I on the way— sitting here, listening, reading, or doing the tasks given to me?"

As I climb I smell the air, see the white caps of the mountains, look at the smiling hikers who pass me—and I feel happy. Now comes the question of the "observer": Am I remembering my-self—the "I" which sees and experiences all this—or am I identified, has "I" disappeared?

I have to clarify this in myself: when do I remember my-self—and when am I identified?

I walk down the mountain and see the snow, the pine trees, the blue sky, with different eyes. My lungs fill with deep—dif-ferent—breaths. I sense the spring in my step and I begin to sing. I know that now *I am*—I remember myself.

This is the beginning of the way. Inside myself I have climbed up the steps in the past months and years—and have reached a plateau. And this is where "the way" begins—with objective self-awareness, with self-remembering.

Chapter 9

Questions

The teaching of Gurdjieff is based on oral transmission, on the interaction of students and teacher. To create this, my teachers time and again stood in front of their groups and asked, "What is *your* question?"

Questions are the life blood of a group meeting. Real questions arise from a deep need and inner search and cannot be created artificially. I have to realize that **I am in question**. Then I may be able to look for "a" question from deep inside me. If I sincerely look, it will come. I may sense it, grope for it, and, if I am fortunate, a discussion that is initiated by my question may lead me to an answer, although it may not be the answer I expect or hope to receive. Many of us, especially when we "manufacture" a question from the wrong place, already have our own answer in mind, and because of this can never hear an answer, even if it is given to us. However, if we are open enough, we can gain much from listening to the question we ask, even a manufactured one. We may discover who asks, and from what level the question came. All of this is valuable.

It is therefore necessary to bring to meetings your own life and Work questions. At times it is important to prepare and ponder on these questions before meeting with your teacher or group. At other times you must try to search in the present moment for that which is *your* question. Observe who is it in you that asks the question. From which "I" does the question arise? Can I actually observe this? What then is a real question?

There are many questions about situations in my life in which I am identified and I can't find my way. Do I have such a question in this instant? There are questions arising from the study

39

of Gurdjieff's teaching, as I begin to try to understand and ver-ify the ideas of the Work he brought. These questions are prac-tical and can lead to useful answers and new beginnings, beginnings toward my inner growth and being.

On the other hand, there are questions that are too big for the level on which I commonly exist. These questions should be saved and returned to time and time again with complete accep-tance of their incompleteness at my level and without recrimi-nation or impatience. For example, the question "Who am I?" is a very big question, but I must not dwell on it to the exclusion of asking questions whose answers I can use as I am, on my level. Moreover, since the question is a very big one, it is ex-tremely hard for me to know when I have received an answer. Instead, I start with smaller, practical questions whose answers are easier to recognize and put into practice *now*, as I am. I search for questions whose answers could lead to growth from the place where I am right now.

At a noon meeting someone composed a very big question. A group leader, looking down from the dais to the questioner at the luncheon table calmly replied, "Be naive when you ask a question." The man who asked the question was so hurt by this answer that he left the group. We must realize that an answer may not meet our expectations and that our sensitivity to our own self-importance may be injured by an objective answer. I must ask myself, "Am I really looking for an answer?"

The big questions, if they are truly our own, can serve as a beacon, though it is possible that as we grow in our work even these beacons can be abandoned. Do I have the courage and pa-tience to stay in front of my questions and just accept the state of not knowing, not understanding?

I wish *to be*. What does this mean to me as I am now? What is my being? For years I asked teachers, authors, and philoso-phers the question, "What is mind?" Many words were spoken to me, but I heard nothing. Eventually it came to me in a quiet sitting: Mind is a force—a tool through which my intellectual or emotional center can communicate with me. If real answers fall on a different place in me, a very quiet place, a sacred place, then an inner transformation can begin. This place is a result of years of preparatory work and is built one brick at a time. My own living questions help form the bricks and mortar of this place.

There are many questions that may arise in me for which I find answers in books, lectures, and "learned persons." But there are still questions in me, questions I can hardly formulate, questions whose presence I can only *feel*, with answers which are beyond my ability to express. How do I find those answers? Again, for me there is but one way—silence, inner quiet, total passivity of the body, "outer" mind and emotion.

If this can be achieved, then something may happen—not an answer through ordinary channels, but I feel the question has been answered. It may lead, then, to other questions. Is it *you* who now knows or is it the daily, ordinary you that "knows"? Is it something in you or of you which exists on a different plane that knows? Can it be that my level is related to the level of my question? Could it be that years of inner work, conscious labor, and intentional suffering have produced a high aim? I remember again the words "I am in question."

Chapter 10

Hearing and Listening

We need finer tools and instruments if we are trying to reach a higher level. We need a different approach, one that only the higher centers can bring us to. I recall the "theme for the day" at a work weekend in Armonk, New York. "Try to **listen** today. You can do this only for brief moments, then you fall asleep again. But you can **hear** often during the day, for moments, if you pay attention to listening." As we practiced this, it was amazing how much I heard: the footsteps of others, the gravel crunching, the leaves of the trees rustling in the wind. I could hear my own breathing, the voices of others when they spoke amongst themselves, and where the voices came from. Some were impatient, some were warm and helpful, and some were completely mechanical. From the voices of the people working around me, I could feel the quality of their attention and, observing this, my own attention was collected again.

I experienced a different listening. My whole organism listened, with its fullest focused attention, since *I* wished to hear every single word that was said. So often we fall into the trap of asking a question of a teacher and formulating our own answer even before the question has been answered, without ever hearing what we are told.

All our lives depend on how well we are able to listen inside. Because of our identification with the "noise" of outer life, we do not hear what our higher centers are constantly telling us. If we only could listen, life would be so much easier for us.

But what does it mean to listen? Listen to whom? Listen to what? Who is listening?

I say, "I wish to hear." First I must ask: "Who wants to hear? Is it an 'I', a group of 'I's', or is it all of me?" Only if it is all of me can my wish materialize. And only if the need is great will it come from the right place. I must listen with my whole being, both inner and outer. I also wish to hear nuances, subtleties, which underlie what goes on around me.

I wish to hear national, racial, geographic, even planetary influences speaking to me. I wish to hear, sense in people's voices who they are, their religious and family background, their education and upbringing, social and domestic circumstances.

I wish to be in touch with my higher centers. I try to make contact with them so that I can begin to hear what they say. To do this, I need to increase my inner sensitivity. The emotional center can feel the inner state of other people, and this is what I want to listen to. I wish to hear my inner self, what my being tells me, to hear the lie in the other person and also the lie in me. When you listen internally, listen with the solar plexus; the mind is only a police officer.

We must be very, very quiet to be able to tune in to finer, higher vibrations. Our normal vibrations are too coarse. Using *the wish*, we try to establish a connection, a way to listen. Once we learn how to listen, we have already achieved a higher state of being. Our organs *know* how to listen. We hear nuances in other people's voices; we have learned to be attuned to the moods of others. We use it in salesmanship, in understanding of and compassion for others, in classroom teaching. But all this is on life's level, though it does point to the fact that we have the capability to listen.

Wrong functioning of the human machine and the lack of connection between the centers used for ordinary life and the two higher centers is the result of insufficient development of the lower centers. It is precisely this lack of development of the lower centers, or their faulty functioning, which prevents us from making contact with our higher centers by truly listening.

We have to listen with the appropriate centers, the intellectual as well as the emotional. When thought is already registered, try to feel. When you feel, try to direct your thought onto your feeling. Until now, our thought and feeling have functioned separately.

It is necessary for real *listening* that my attention be centered. It is only when you are centered that you gather your attention, so that you will be able to focus on what you are trying to listen to and allow the meaning to come into you. This is described in the Teaching as "the collected state."

To hear, I have to use my mind to quiet my thoughts and direct my thinking into a different channel. I try to remain in the state of internal immobility I acquired in my sitting. This is my aim: to live the Work, to think from work. I consecrate a definite time during each day to have the sensation of my body, to be present and quiet, and, most of all, to remember this aim.

I start this in the morning exercise, when I try to attain total quiet. I have to observe the quality of my sitting, my sincerity in the wish to be quiet. I have to see when I lie to myself about this quality. When does my attention wander? It is when the "debil" (the word Gurdjieff used for the devil) tempts me, injecting thoughts of the coming day and its emotional involvements, the inner noise, which makes real hearing impossible.

Little by little, inner sensitivity increases, the "receiving apparatus" becomes fine-tuned, and I begin to hear. "Make a space inside you to be able to hear," I was told by my teachers. Something is drawn to this vacuum. It may only be a word or a taste. From that place, we can hear what we do not normally hear. We can hear the silence.

You can and do reach this state occasionally in your morning exercise, when you allow yourself to listen. My listening can achieve results in two different ways. First, I listen for answers entering from the outside, understanding, help coming from above. Second, I try to hear how my higher centers are guiding me.

Learning to listen and hear was a milestone on the path toward my aim, the perfecting of the higher being bodies, and indispensable in facing my Gurdjieff groups in Colorado. When I answer their questions, it is not from my personal knowledge, but from listening to the higher centers for the answers. I believe in the power of higher centers. I believe the higher centers do have access to higher knowledge, greater understanding, and are able to contact the "inner circle of humanity" which balances the cosmos. I include in my daily prayers: "I wish to **listen** that I may **hear**. I wish to **see** that I may **be**."

Chapter 11

External Considering

You are around a person who has been ill for a long time. Again and again, you may hear this person speak of wishing to "crawl into a hole," preferring to die, being useless, or being forgotten after his or her death. Society, life, your own inclination calls for consideration, caring, kindness. But the Work demands more from you. It teaches you to put yourself into that person's place. Attempt to sense his or her pain, despair, hopelessness. Try to understand this negativity and these feelings about the injustice and unfairness of life. Try to understand and cope with his or her pent-up anger and resentment.

You try to exercise patience and compassion. However, after a time, you get bored hearing complaint after complaint. You get angry, affected by the drawn, sad expression of the person who is ill. As hard as you try to live the Work, to practice external considering, your effort will become only lip service.

At this moment, become aware of the *need* of the person with your whole being. Then, something may open up in you, something new touches you. A light is turned on in the dark room where you are. You see the furniture, the paintings on the wall, the carpet. You see internally the misery of the sick person. You feel it reaching out to you. It is as though a veil is removed and you are confronted with the reality of a human being's suffering. You begin to understand what Mr. Gurdjieff taught us about external considering.

External considering does not stand alone. It has its opposite living next to it. It is called internal considering—my own inner mechanical reaction to a situation. To be aware of my internal considering requires an "inner seeing" in which I observe my reaction toward a situation. This must occur before I am able to *act* outwardly. Then I am less identified and free to act in accordance with the teachings of the Work. Doing this, not only do I help the other person, but I help myself. I have to prepare my inner attitude first before I can exercise external considering.

I am unable to practice external considering before having made contact with my inner situation. I have to see my impatience, unwillingness to exert myself, resistance toward putting myself in the place of the sufferer, as well as my own feelings in the situation, my selfishness, my laziness—and eventually, if I am really honest with myself, my indifference. When I *see* all this in myself, when I can *accept* this picture of myself, only then am I ready for external considering.

External considering needs to be practiced each day if I wish to *live* the Work. In life, you may have to consider the mood of a prospective customer, the attitude of a client, the demands made upon you in any business or personal situation. You have to consider your co-workers, your superiors, your subordinates. You have to consider the members of your family, your wife, your children, and even the relatives you don't like. Why? Because you need to constantly practice what the Work teaches if you wish to grow and develop your psychological body. The law of three enters here when you see two opposite emotions and find them reconciled in an appropriate action.

Up to this moment, you were in the lowest, mechanical part of your intellectual or emotional center. Then a deeper understanding begins to arise in you and that understanding becomes your guide. This is my own experience. It is as if I were going behind the scenery in a theater and into the life behind the performance on the stage.

What I am trying to express is the depth of understanding of our experience. The surface is not enough, and we have no idea of the dimensions behind the surface. It opens a new perspective, allows an influx of new energy, and compels me to make a new effort. It shows how much farther I must go and how shallow a level I'm really on. External considering forces me out of myself. I "see" the lives of others and in turn I begin to see myself. This is how external considering works.

Chapter 12

Attention

It is 2:00 A.M. Bully and I have arrived at an unoccupied chalet way up in the Austrian Alps. We sleep on straw-covered boards facing the ascent of the Ortler, the highest mountain in the range.

Before dawn we are ready, with crampons, ice axes, a 30-meter rope to start out with, and two lanterns to show us the trail under the starry night. The first part of the climb is a canyon of sheer ice, between two towering rock walls. One thousand feet ahead of us is the most dangerous part—"Stein Schlag"—with rocks careening from above when the sun hits the top at about 6:00 A.M.

We are not roped together. On the sheer ice edge where we are climbing there is no way of securing the other in case a rock hits him. There is only you, your crampons, the ice ax, and your attention, which is fiercely focused toward the top from where the rocks come whistling down. Climbing along the edge of this canyon of ice you know you are unable to avoid the rocks from above by jumping out of the way.

We make it to the top of the ravine. A flat plateau laced with crevasses a thousand feet deep and 15 to 20 feet wide is our next obstacle. The sun is up, warming our bodies, and snow is glittering in thousands of crystals. In front of us lay the crevasses yawning in a beautiful turquoise and changing to a darker and darker blue into bottomless black.

We start to rope on and tackle the first one: the abyss connected with a snow bridge. Our attention is at its peak; a false move, shifting weights, could mean certain death. Will it hold me? Is it firm enough that early in the morning? Because I am lighter, Bully jams his ice pick into the snow and wraps the rope around it to "belay" me. I believe he prays.

I test the bridge. I don't trust it with my weight concentrated on my feet. I want to spread it over a wider surface. What to do? Lie down on my stomach and slowly, slowly inch myself over the gaping crevasse. I make it—and so does Bully, me belaying him from the other side of the gap, hardly daring to breath until he has mastered the gap.

We use the word *attention* so often in our inner work; we hear it in meetings and see it in the literature of Gurdjieff's teachings. Have we ever tried to see what it really means? We use the word in so many forms, but what is attention, really? I see it as a force related to energy. It is a quality of awareness. Attention is like a powerful searchlight illuminating my inner and outer situation. It is like a chemical which separates other chemicals in our organism into individual substances, identifying what they are and enabling us to deal with each individually.

Focused, directed attention allows me to hear what my centers tell me, to see myself and my problems as objectively as possible, uninfluenced by imagination or even by the teaching. It can reveal the "I" which I am at the moment, cutting through the illusions that I have of myself. It allows me to produce the total inner quietness needed for the transformation of what I am into what I wish to be, for reaching a higher state. I see attention as a force which gathers and focuses some of my scattered energies into one place, like a laser beam, or a magnifying lens focusing light. Attention can also be a force which helps create and increase the energy I need to carry out a task or a project, whether it is regarding an everyday situation, a personal psychological problem, or an esoteric observation needed in my search.

How can I use attention as a support for my three major centers? I can direct my attention to the sensation of my body. I can use attention to work on my mind, by focusing on the thoughts that spin off associations, taking me along in their wake. I say, "thoughts are not thinking," because they are different. By focusing attention on my thoughts and attempting to calm them, I allow what I call the higher mind to guide and help me to make contact with a force descending from above.

Attention helps me to differentiate between thoughts, thinking, and feeling. Realize how very valuable this is, for so often we use our intellectual center when the solution lies in our feelings. How often are we carried away by the emotions when clear intellect is needed. Attention is the ray which cuts through the cobwebs obscuring my path and shows me the kind of energy to use—intellectual, emotional, or physical.

Attention helps me deal with my laziness and direct my energies "to make efforts." Effort, energy and attention are intimately connected. But I need to realize how they are obtained. I collect and focus my attention then I summon the energies to finally make the effort. What effort? This is the point where we hear Gurdjieff's call to conscious labor and intentional suffering.

• • • •

A student came to a venerable Roshi in Japan. He prostrated himself before him and asked: "Master, what is the most valuable word you can give me for my self-development?" The Roshi was silent for a while, then looked at the student and said: "Attention."

The student hesitated, pondered for a while, then spoke up again, "Thank you Roshi, what would be the next most valuable advice?" The Roshi pondered, raised his head again, and replied: "Attention."

The student was puzzled, hesitated, and asked again, "What is the third thing I should focus on in my endeavors to raise my state?"

"Attention," answered the Roshi.

Chapter 13

Food

Mrs. Pearce told me that at one time Mr. Gurdjieff took a group on an outing in the Swiss Alps. When he noticed his pupils involved in admiring the scenery as they sat down to lunch, he made the point, "When you eat, *eat*. When you look, *look*." I have such a vivid recollection of practicing this when I went hiking with one of my students in the Colorado mountains. We drove from Denver, over Guanella Pass at 12,000 feet, to the trailhead of Silver Dollar Lake. The day was sparkling and crisp at this altitude, under the blue sky, with the mountains crowned by clouds and capped by snow. The meadows were covered with Alpine flowers. When we reached a plateau overlooking Emerald Lake, it was the perfect place for lunch for two weary hikers.

We took off our backpacks, got out our sandwiches, a thermos of coffee, and cold drinks, and began to feast. But Mr. Gurdjieff's words came to us as a reminder. Surrounded by all this beauty, we ate, ate consciously, aware of the taste, the sensation of our bodies, as well as of our food and what it meant—nourishment of the planetary body. Only after our lunch did we again consciously turn to the second and third being foods, the air and the impressions of our surroundings. I truly felt they were a more vital food than the lunch we ate because they fed something higher in us than the bodies sitting on these rocks.

Man requires three kinds of food: our ordinary food, air, and impressions.

The first being food is our ordinary food which gives us physical nourishment. Be present to yourself when eating. Try to get optimum value out of your meals. We should not eat like automatons or, worse still, read while we eat. The value of your physical food will decrease if you read a newspaper, magazine, or book, or watch TV while eating your meals. If you prepare your food, give it more value by preparing it consciously with the intention of serving the best possible meal. I commented after a meal at one of our work weekends, "What made this such an exceptionally good dinner? It was prepared with love."

The second type of food is air. It is not the deep breath of fresh air which is "the food," however; it is the cosmic substances you take in through your lungs and pores when breathing. These substances in the air must be in proper proportions to facilitate the growth of the Kesdjan body. In baking bread, only the right proportion of flour and water will produce the right kind of dough.

The third being food must also be properly understood. What are impressions? They are material, as everything in the cosmos is material. They are vibrations that touch our centers and combine with their own vibrations, to enhance, refine and increase their frequency, until they become suitable food for the third body, the real "I." You see a beautiful sunset, a starry night, smell the pungent aroma of pine trees, the delicate fragrance of a flower, the salty breeze coming from the sea shore. You enjoy the taste of a good meal, the touch of a lovely skin. All these are impressions, food for the third being body.

I receive this food when I consciously read a book that expands my knowledge and touches my being. I can receive it when I attend a lecture, a concert or a good meeting. When I walk on a snowy trail and stop to see the countless crystals in the sunlight, reflecting blue, orange, green, always changing depending on the angle from which I look, I marvel, "Is this not food?" I don't know and I really don't have to know. I only feel that "something" enters into me, giving me a lift, up to a different level. Food is when I am touched in a way that helps me to enter a higher state.

These are *impressions*, which are the substance of this food. Conscious labor and intentional suffering helps us to digest this food and build and crystallize our higher being bodies. Super-efforts must be attempted. Try to do the impossible!

You must try to absorb this and be conscious of all three foods—as often during the day as you can—on your own level of being. I sense my body when I set the breakfast table. In fact, I am aware of all my senses, aware of my hands holding the coffee cup, aware of the warmth of it, of the aroma of the coffee, tasting the deliciousness of it. I hear the bubbling sounds of water boiling and look at the room, seeing it in a different way. It becomes three-dimensional; furniture, pictures, the carpet, all appear as if I had never seen them before. I feel, I see, I smell, I taste, because I am aware, awake, and I realize by contrast how often I am asleep to all this, when my attention is not gathered.

This, and my morning exercise which precedes it, is the prelude and direction for the day, in which "I wish to *live the Work*."

Chapter 14

Higher Being Bodies

Throughout the ages people have believed in the possibility of evolution by working on and developing finer bodies than the one given at birth. Different teachings attached various names to these higher bodies and classified them in four categories. Christian teaching called the first body the carnal body, the second body the natural body, the third body the spiritual body, and the fourth body the divine body. Theosophy calls the four bodies the physical body, the astral body, the mental body and the causal body. Mr. Gurdjieff uses terms taken from Eastern stories about man, the carriage (our planetary body), the horse (the feelings, emotions), the driver (intellect, mind) and the master (conscious mind, will, single "I").

We are instructed to perfect our second body first, crystallize it, before working on the others. However, the same food nourishes all four bodies, only in different proportions. This food consists of our regular daily food, air and impressions. While the first is understood, air as food needs some explanation. I took it literally when the teachings said, "Air is the second Being Food," with our regular nourishment the first, and impressions the third. Only later I understood its meaning. It is not the air we inhale but the "cosmic substances" transmitted to us through the air which help build the second Being Body. How much food we take out of it depends on our inner development and the level of our being. Mr. Gurdjieff mentioned to his pupils that they take five substances of food with one breath while he takes in ninety. He also cautioned those who expect to gain increased power by means of breath control. He said that they are foolish to try unless they go through long preliminary training under a qualified teacher, because they interfere with functions which, if interfered with long enough, might never work normally afterwards.

Gurdjieff taught that the perfection of the second being body is accomplished by conscious labor and intentional suffering (internally). Breathing transmits planetary influences and even emanations from the Sun Absolute, from the cosmos (externally). Breathing consciously; that is, observing the breathing and being aware of the processes described, is the right direction toward our aim. Through conscious labor and intentional suffering, through very hard work for a very long time, we are able to build the higher being bodies, one after another, perfecting the second body first and higher ones only after the second is crystallized. Conscious breathing has other benefits as well. It has the power to change the energies in us. It is even possible to regulate our emotional state when we breathe with awareness.

I try to be conscious of my breathing in my waking hours and asked one of my teachers and was told, "To my knowledge, no special breathing exercises were included in Gurdjieff's method of inner perfection. The method is not *breathing*, but development of an acute inner sensation.

"If one observes breathing, one notes that its rhythm changes as one's inner state changes. But as one becomes interested in watching the breathing, something tries to change it. It is difficult to observe and not to interfere. The aim is to go deeper and deeper into what appears first as silence—to hear, see, sense what lies *beyond* this silence. Until the three lower centers are in harmony it is impossible for us to do this intentionally. One may and does have flashes—over shorter and longer periods—of this state after many years, to varying degrees, but nothing lasting will come about unless one approaches this exercise without any desire for results, but only, with humility, 'to be able.' It is only in this direction that I can understand that the meaning of life is not to achieve something, but to learn to sense the presence of higher powers coming from above."

Chapter 15

Anger

One of the most frequent discussions in my groups concerns anger. From where does anger come? What is the cause and what are the symptoms? How can I handle it? What can I do about it?

Anger is an emotion connected with *violence* and is one of the most destructive emotions to our being. We can observe anger by seeing its manifestations. These appear as an inner tenseness, a jittery feeling, a queasiness in the stomach, or an accelerated heartbeat. It can be a heated feeling in the head. Sometimes we can pinpoint its origin.

There is at least one object of anger, either tangibly present or imagined. There is the "myself" who is angry. Thus anger can be viewed either externally, in relation to an object, or psychologically, in relation to "myself." If you can be scrupulously sincere with yourself, you may observe in which center your anger originates. Realize that many emotions simply dissolve, evaporate, if observed objectively.

Anger can originate outside of us in life. We get angry when we do not get our way, do not get what we want. This is internal considering. We are identified with the situation and the person. At times we can painfully recognize that the cause of anger lies within ourselves. Internal considering is always identification and therefore mechanical. External considering, on the other hand, is conscious.

We can become angry when our vanity has been hurt, by someone's words, an accusation, or an implied insult. How do you face the anger caused by this? We have been told, "**Nothing**

57

is harder to bear than the negative manifestations of others toward you." Putting this into practice, it becomes a work exercise of voluntary suffering. Try to detach yourself, try to create "space" within yourself and recognize this as an opportunity to really "*do* the Work." The insult hurts. But isn't it of much greater value to realize at that moment that *now* is your opportunity to grow; *now* you can take a step toward a higher level?

A method for dealing with anger begins with recognizing and seeing anger objectively. Look at it from different angles. However, as an emotion, anger will ultimately need to be handled emotionally when it is the most deep-seated kind.

You can work on anger through the body. This is the easiest method to deal with it for us, for it is something we can do as we are. Jog around the block, play tennis, clean house, polish the silver or furniture, get on your bike or take a brisk walk. Work up a sweat. Increase your circulation and intake of oxygen through deep breathing. Observe the exhalation of your breath and see that your lungs are completely emptied. Working physically, the energy your anger has created can be transformed into a positive force that consumes, absorbs the anger, and when you have ended your physical exercise the anger may have dissolved itself, like a chemical in water.

The more difficult situation is when anger lies in an emotional upheaval and is not completely erased by physical effort. Again, you must *see* it first. In this case you can, in addition to trying the physical exercise mentioned above, engage the intellect by asking yourself, "Does it lie in my past? If so, must I carry it into this present moment? Is this trend of thought or emotion useful? Can't I be 'here and now' instead of dwelling on a past wrong, a wrong which cannot be made right any more?" "Here and now" I can substitute, consciously, intentionally, a different feeling—forgiveness, a canceling out.

Margaret Anderson, in her book *The Unknowable Gurdjieff*, recalls how she was angry and rebellious about everything that

Mr. Gurdjieff asked her to do. "Conscious labor" was too difficult, "voluntary suffering" too unendurable to undertake. And then, in one enlightened moment, she had a picture of herself, her state, and its cause. She rushed to the Rue des Colonels Renard, to Gurdjieff's apartment, and said, "Mr. Gurdjieff, I see now that it was because of my vanity and self-love that I was so angry."

Finally, when dealing with anger, you can go to your quiet inner place. Sit down, relax your body. Observe your breathing. Observe and try to still your thoughts, your emotions—engage all three centers. Create this state and **allow something to happen**. At times the best way is to change nothing and simply watch and see.

Chapter 16

Tension

It was a blustery winter night, and the blizzard had dumped 12 inches of snow on Denver. The snow plows were laboring and most drivers were staying at home that night when we gathered at the home of a student to meet with Mrs. W., who had flown in from San Francisco. Inside it was warm, the fireplace spread a glow on the group, sitting in a circle around Mrs. W., creating a wonderful setting for her message.

I was sitting next to Mrs. W., a very prominent person in the Work. It was a small, intimate meeting. She spoke on tensions, but as she talked she radiated a relaxed calmness and serenity to which my body and mind responded in a surprising fashion.

I have practiced and observed relaxation for many years in my morning exercises, in most of my sittings, in leading my groups. However, sitting next to her, I realized a different quality of calmness in me. It was a physical experience. I felt it in the outside muscles of my eyes, around my mouth, then slowly it went deeper, permeating my entire organism. There was a sweetness in this experience which stayed with me for a long time.

Tension is a disease. It creates a constant drain of energy. This needs to be seen. The word "dis-ease" itself gives me a clue about how to cope with it, where to search. It affects the whole system, although it manifests itself in different parts at different times. I see that there is no *ease*. I can observe it in my head, when a problem goes round and round, preoccupying my mental capacities. At times I seem unable to break out of this vicious circle.

It can manifest itself in my muscles, especially around the neck and shoulders, which become as taut as wires. At other times, tension holds my solar plexus or my throat in a vise, manipulating my breathing until it feels that I am almost choking. It interferes with my digestion, my appetite, and even my sex. Tension may come as an indication that I have not "cleared accounts." It may indicate that I am worrying or that I am ill at ease with my surroundings and lack confidence. It may indicate that I listen to external life, and that I use life to arrive at a valuation of my self, all of me. Tension is a precursor of mechanical anger and impatience. There is no impatience or mechanical anger that is relaxed. All of this contributes to the tension which lies in me, and if I observe myself honestly I will be able to see this.

How do I recognize tension? Often I am not aware that I am tense. I can begin by noticing my body; this is something that we all can do. Are your jaws clenched, are your leg muscles tight, or are the muscles around your eyes and lips drawn? Do I see that I make a fist, that my fingers are like claws, or that I pace up and down? Each of us has noticeable characteristics which can tell us when we are tense. If you find it difficult to determine them, ask a person who knows you well what are the external manifestations of your tension.

Tension manifests itself also in the intellect and in the emotions. Depending on where they reside, my tensions can be eased using the intellectual, emotional or physical center. I can take a walk, jog, play a game of tennis or racquetball, practice Tai Chi or similar methods taught in the East. I can read, listen to music, or turn to myself. I must try to observe which kind of tension I am under at this moment. I detach myself from the situation, to see myself objectively and not be submerged in my present state. From this more objective level, I can select the appropriate method to deal with my tension.

Relaxation is a key. I must make an effort to get out of the state of tension instead of wallowing in it (which only increases the tension). I see the enormous damage tension does to me, to my body, my spiritual life, my inner growth. I see in all this how my energy, my spiritual life blood, is drained. This must be stopped as if my life depended on it. On the spiritual or esoteric level, tension prevents me from practicing "inner listening."

We practice relaxation in our sittings and meditation—the flow of energy through the limbs, the abdomen, the torso, the head and face muscles. The teaching and practice of having the sensation of the body is very important. This practice helps refine and strengthen the faculty of being able to radiate quietness. To fight tension, we must create total outer quiet, which in turn will create a similar inner relaxation.

That snowy evening with Mrs. W. was a challenging experience. It was challenging in that it provided an incentive for increased efforts in relaxation. It showed me how much more was possible. It was also a shock. How was it possible that I had rarely observed myself in a state of relaxation that was as deep as this experience? How was it that I did not remember that the quality of my many previous attempts to relax was not what it could be, and that much more could be achieved?

Chapter17

Fear

I recall some very revealing insights when our groups had several discussions about fear. I remember how the theme unfolded itself, how people looked deeply into themselves, how many different fears came into the daylight.

There was someone who had been silent in the group for months. All of a sudden, the dam broke and he described how he was repressed and abused by his contemporaries as a child. He spoke of how defenseless he felt and how he withdrew into himself, built a protective shell around himself out of fear of being hurt, and finally how the Work and the group support gave him the courage to see himself and his fear and to bring it into the open. It was wonderful to see the relief in his face, in his eyes, when he described it.

Another student had several talks privately with me in which she cried, in great distress and unhappiness. Disappointment in previous relationships had caused great pain and withdrawal. She did not quite see that fear based in the past was being brought into the present and was causing it all. When we discussed fear in the meeting, her eyes lit up all of a sudden and you could see courage entering—because an angle had been found from which the past could be seen, opening possibilities for the future. She then recognized the meaning of Gurdjieff's words when he said, "Live here and now."

A basic deep-rooted fear was vividly described by another student. He spoke about a dream of being on the top floor of a building and opening a door which led to the roof. He found himself surrounded by threatening high-rise buildings which closed in on him. The edge of the roof represented a six-story drop. He described his dread of going near the edge and was consciously aware of his fear. This was of value—to *see* the fear. In fact, at the end of the description of this occurrence he felt the possibility of making the additional effort, the next time, to go to the edge.

There are overwhelming, draining, corroding fears caused by fantasies, projections of future events, dread of catastrophes that may befall yourself or your friends or loved ones. For example, you may fear the weather, that a snowstorm or tornado will interfere with your important plans for business or pleasure. Or you may worry that your children may contract a fatal illness. How many times do these imagined events materialize? Rarely, if ever.

When I pondered on fear, I tried to connect it with what the Work teaches us about deep, inner observation. The first thought entering my mind was "the fear of the unknown." But what part of the unknown? The part of a man that he is afraid to see in himself. You may be afraid to see a reality that does not live up to the illusion you have of yourself. This image would be jeopardized if you really saw yourself the way you are. This fear may be the same fear that we experience in seeing our vanity and wounded pride. This is the fear that you won't be able to bear the disappointment if you see yourself objectively.

These are inner, psychological fears. But there are others. You can be afraid of being asked for more and greater efforts in the Work. You can fear that your routine, your laziness, will be shaken up. You can fear that your conscience will make itself known. Our two greatest enemies, feelings of inadequacy and rejection, are there, waiting to surface and create a fear which can be conquered with long work in a group.

We have spoken mainly about useless fears. However, there are fears—call them biological fears—which are warranted. Useful fears arise when I have to walk through a park known to be dangerous. There are fears giving rise to cautious driving on icy roads. If I find myself hiking above the timber line during a thunder storm or blinding snow storm, there is a natural fear. These are legitimate, useful fears. These are fears that tell me "Now I must be awake."

In every situation in our life, there are at least two angles from which you can observe two groups of "I's" acting in you. There is the negative side, which is the fear itself, the mechanical worrying. But look at the opposite side. What is the opposite of *fear*? It is **courage**. It takes great courage to see all this in you—not to turn away, but face it. Do you realize that by having the courage to make the effort to see you tap and build within yourself different energies, energies which can help you in your inner transformation, energies which will ultimately help you in conquering your fears? Remember the law of three.

What can I do about my fears? What action can I take to cope with them? I can try to be conscious in facing my emotion when fear creeps in. I can try to become aware of it entering and how it manifests itself. Little by little, this seeing may clarify my feelings and diminish at least the fears based on imagination.

Chapter 18

Negativity

As I awake, I have a vague feeling of discontent. I curse the driver in front of me for moving too slowly. I raise my voice at my children. Seated at my desk, I stare into space as depression immobilizes me. Filled with rage and frustration, I find myself at the borderline of insanity. All of these occurrences share the same attribute, negativity. I try to see my negativity and search for its inner source.

I can find many causes if I look outside myself. But there can be no outside cause for those of us who are in the Gurdjieff Work. An outside event may trigger negativity, but we must be aware, painful as this realization is, that the cause of negativity lies in us alone. Its real origin is in one of our centers, and therefore we have to talk to each center in its own language. Negativity always begins in the instinctive center and is present before the emotional or intellectual center knows that it exists.

Let us assume negativity manifests itself in an emotion. No intellectual arguments will be of help. The "horse," our emotional center, does not understand the language of the intellectual center. On the other hand, if an intellectual process creates negativity, we can probe and reason with our mind. The moving center, too, has its own laws, under which negativity can be recognized, observed, and dissolved like a chemical substance. Having practiced self-observation as it was taught from the beginning in the Work, I know the first step in dealing with negativity is **inner separation**. I have to *see* myself—myself as I am, and not the image I have of myself. As I learn this, I learn to separate or distance myself from myself. I begin to see the many "I's" which contain me. Eventually I will find the ones which want to keep me in bondage and the ones which can help me. I can observe how identified or submerged I really am. I have to step back and create a space between the situation and myself. Once I am truly aware of this, I am able to look for tools to use in confronting and defying my negativity. The foremost is:

DO NOT EXPRESS

NEGATIVE EMOTIONS.

This is the key. If you express your negative emotions, you are in their power. As you hear yourself expressing them, your inner alarm clock will alert you to "switch the direction of your thoughts." If you miss this moment, the momentum takes over and the opportunity is lost.

This is a time when the intellectual center can influence the emotional center. It is the one moment in which you still have the power to deflect negative emotions by intentionally directing your mind away from this obsession. Ask yourself, "Is this *useful?*" By "this" I mean the negativity that is enveloping you. Think differently, the Work says; that means "think from the Work." Implement the ideas of the Work. You can then engage one or more centers, depending on what type of person you are and what the circumstances require.

Man number one can go for a walk, a hike or a jog. You may want to take a bicycle ride or practice your favorite sport if you are this type. Man number two can sculpt, knit, paint, play a musical instrument, or go to an art museum. Man number three can turn to his library or bookstore, write an essay, solve a puzzle. This re-direction of energy "absorbs" the negativity and the energy is siphoned out of the negativity itself and projected into the activity.

I find it very useful, especially if I think I am too tired to work, to turn to my diaries, which I have compiled in the forty years I have been in the Work. I open any one of them at random (maybe "something" guides me to the right page, directing me to suitable help in this moment) and I experience an influx of new energy. My laziness evaporates, a new interest enters and takes the place of the insidious negativity which had tried to creep up on me. Do you have activities that you can use in such moments? Find and chose your own to help in changing your inner state or mood.

The state that negativity creates can always be influenced, turned around by *efforts*, be they physical, mental or emotional. Efforts create energy; negativity depletes and destroys it. We are negative in self-indulgence, self-pity, making accounts, not forgiving imaginary wrongs. We become negative by allowing others—or our own thoughts, memories, and recollections—to ruin our day. We become apprehensive, fearful about something which lies in the future, most of the time in our fantasy or imagination, something which in all probability will never occur.

Negativity can be produced by illness. The sufferer feels he or she is entitled to be discouraged. Financial difficulties, family upheavals, loss of a job, all can create negativity. This is a serious disease which we want to recognize and fight. It is a big task and one of the biggest in our daily lives. We must confront all the things that make us negative and summon the help available, the help which is in each of us, the help the Work can and will give us. If I realize that I am in prison, I must try to escape from it—and I can.

Now we have to try to see the hidden negativities. If you curse quietly under your breath at someone or something, this too is expressing negativity. A subtle frown, making the usual hopeless gesture with your hand, letting your shoulders droop, sighing—all this has to be watched, seen, observed, and categorized properly as expressing negativity. Restlessness may express it, because its cause may lie in negativity. Such subtle expressions of negativity are unlimited in number and must be observed most carefully to catch our negativity in whatever form it manifests itself and as early as possible. We observe the endless dialogues going round and round in us, accusing, complaining, justifying, and we ask, "Is this internal conversation useful?" This phrase has helped me in many situations where mind or emotions or both had gotten ahold of me. When I realized it, I had to grin and say, "What a fool am I!"

All I have written now are symptoms, reasons and tangible causes for negativity. What I have not touched on are moods—the states which enter me, so vague, so undefined, and yet nevertheless so obsessive and powerful. These are states where I have no handle, where I seem helpless and lost. How can I cope with these?

I have pondered, speculated and I am still helpless and searching for a concrete answer. I think, "I must just let go, allow them to exist in me, don't try to fight them, but realize this is life, this is the rhythm of life, the law-conformable ups and downs we must accept until a '**do**' arises which will bring the law of seven back on track."

At that moment, life can begin anew.

Chapter 19

Impatience

You are pacing back and forth, tapping your fingers on the table, whipping your feet up and down. You feel something creeping into your stomach. You sense a tingling sensation in your forehead. Your breathing changes, but even though you take some deep, slow breaths, thinking you might control it, "it" takes over. Your breathing accelerates and almost stifles you, you can't get enough air into your lungs, your solar plexus starts quivering. You are impatient. All your motions and emotions are three times as fast as in your ordinary state.

Is this the time when the emotional center begins to take over from the moving center? You begin to probe, subconsciously first, then consciously, for the cause, the root, of the impatience. Pictures form, phrases come to mind and repeat themselves, over and over again. Your mind is an engine, running in a circle, and the words always return to the beginning of the thought process.

Impatience is an emotion, a destructive emotion which is connected with a time element in us. It is a quality, a characteristic, which makes us wish that events would take place faster or sooner. It prevents us from living in the present. We wish that people talking to us would come to the point, that the job would be done in a shorter time. "I wish morning would come," we complain during a sleepless night. "I wish my guests would arrive before dinner is spoiled." In all these examples there is a time element.

Ego and self-importance will also create impatience in me. Because I am who I am, everyone should be at my beck and call, they should not keep me waiting, they should execute my

70

wishes at once. I am the professor, the physician, the lawyer, the professional, the specialist. I expect people to understand and respect me because of my position, authority and obvious superiority.

This is one type of impatience. Another type is more subtle. It appears as an irritation which I see but I do nothing about. In fact, I like it and consider it a virtue. I take pride in being "efficient," a "doer," and an "accomplisher" of things. I enjoy my negativity. I enjoy the state, in spite of knowing how destructive it may be.

Since impatience is an emotion, understanding of it should naturally come from the emotional center—to be specific, from the intellectual part of the emotional center. Impatience is a manifestation of a negative emotion. Is impatience useful? It is not useful for you or for the Work. From the point of view of the Work, impatience is a leakage of energy, energy which would be so much more valuable if I applied it for my inner development. Try to eliminate it. To do this you try to find the root of your impatience. This does not necessarily imply that you can tackle it immediately. That may not be possible if the root is too deeply buried in you. Your alternative is to begin chipping away at it whenever you see it. Observe it objectively and then use the tools the Work has shown you. Uproot it, chop off the branches of the tree called impatience.

If you are frequently able to observe your impatience, you may catch something which is on the surface, not yet deeply buried. I do this time and again, for weeks. Slowly, something else takes over, something organic within me. It is not the mind any more which tells me, "I am again impatient." There seems to begin an almost chemical reaction, a rejection of this poisonous emotion. The organism itself seems to produce an antidote. The inner tempo slows. Impatience is a fast action—or reaction—and this slower tempo allows me to summon the help the Work has taught us.

How do I slow my inner tempo? Mrs. Pearce said, "Sense your body, sense your feet on the ground." Somehow this makes contact. What kind of contact? I don't know. There was a magic in these words, in what they evoked in me. I feel it even today, after twenty-odd years. Yes, I do sense my body, my feet. Time slows. I have the time needed to create the vacuum, the space in which the Work asserts itself and shows me how to deal with the problem, with my impatience. I can do it. There is a chemistry, a vibration, an influence from higher sources. The impatience loses its grip on me and dissolves like a cloud in the sky. I am free again.

You can use impatience as an alarm clock. When in an impatient state, try to hear your voice. As soon as you do, change its tone and speed. Lower the tone and speed. This we *can* do.

Finally, I can meet it directly. Impatience is a devil, so meet the devil head on. Conquering impatience and developing patience is work on will. "I wish to be," ". . . to have will," ". . . to 'can do'," but first I must try to face the impatience and the negative "I's" which occupy me. Work discipline will allow me to change the direction of my thoughts, giving me a useful aim. I pursue this aim and, in this one instance, I have conquered my impatience. From here on, it is practice, self-observation, and practice, practice again.

It was once said, "I am impatient. I wish to give up my search for sensation in order to do something else, but I can see this and gradually learn to stay in front of my *impatience* until an emotion of patience appears. So long as both emotions are there together, there is struggle between patience and impatience, which speeds up and begins to balance the centers. When this balance takes place, it may become possible for higher conscious energy to pass down into me."

I remember Lord Pentland's words,

"QUIET, QUIET."

In the vibration of his voice I recognized, felt where it came from, and I still hear it today. These words reverberate in me, they make me sense my entire body, they quiet my mind, my emotions, and allow something else to take place. I am "here and now."

Chapter 20

Thoughts Are Not Thinking

I had two phone calls today, both about the same difficulty. "My head is buzzing with thoughts continually," was the first call. The second call described a similar difficulty. A negative thought entered her mind. It went round and round. She tried to stop it, realizing the great leak of energy this was, but it was of no avail. It was like a phonograph record playing over and over, an endless recurrence. She was helpless and discouraged.

I tried to explain to each of the callers the mechanics of the mind in one sentence: **Thoughts are not thinking**.

Where do thoughts originate? How do they enter the mind? We do not know. They are stored associatively and triggered by other thoughts and released not by *thinking* but by a mechanical process of association. The same process that stores, releases them. What we can do with thoughts is to see them as they begin and come into view. If we do this, we have several alternatives. If the thought is valuable to you and to your work, think it through consciously and intentionally. If not, direct your mind into different channels. You might try the alphabet exercise*, which is always profitable and also increases your ability to concentrate. It certainly will fend off unwanted thoughts, because we cannot have two thoughts simultaneously without extraordinary efforts of attention. What always helps me is to ask myself, "Is this thought useful?"

---

* You start the alphabet: A-B-C-D, then go back D-C-B-A. Start with the next letter B-C-D-E and back E-D-C-B. Continue in this way until W-X-Y-Z. At this point go backwards to the beginning in the same way; that is, Z-Y-X-W, W-X-Y-Z, Y-X-W-V, V-W-X-Y, until the beginning is reached.

A thought is like a cloud or wisp entering my mind. It is a word, phrase, image, or sound which takes center stage in the mind's "field of vision." It may originate in a fragrance, a feeling, a sound, a visualization or a memory that is brought to life. Thoughts also come from different "I's" that either initiate the thought or are brought to life by the thoughts. They are passive. On the other hand, thinking is an active, conscious (in the sense that Gurdjieff uses the word), voluntary act unlike the recurrent circular nature of thoughts. Thinking creates a spiral which is driven toward an aim. It is something that "**I**" do and not something that "*it*" does. It is something that engages the intellectual center through effort and the results of my work. Once a thought becomes an emotion, it becomes difficult to destroy.

Thoughts enter uncontrolled. They come from one part of the intellectual center that is called the formatory apparatus. This is the mechanical part of the intellectual center. Each of our regular centers are divided into moving, intellectual and emotional parts. The formatory apparatus' function is to register, catalog, and memorize. It not designed to make decisions or "think" for the whole of me.

The person who wishes to be master of himself or herself will try to differentiate between "thinking" and "thoughts" and try to think thoughts. Try to observe the mind to see what is going on there now. When I succeed in rightly observing my thoughts, without judgment, this state of observation creates the possibility of actively directing the thoughts. This is thinking. Active directed thought leads in turn to conscious thinking and transformation.

I went on a mountain hike after these conversations with my students, to ponder their questions about thoughts and thinking. My first commitment was to empty my mind. It took me over thirty minutes and it was a tremendous struggle. The mind, the "debil," did not give me peace. Thought after thought entered and only after I arrived at the top did I succeed with great difficulty in harnessing my thoughts. I sat down and quiet came. I entered a different state and found myself connected with the Work with my entire being. I was in command of my intellectual center. I could think. I could remain quiet.

Thoughts come at random and mechanically from everywhere. Thoughts "happen." Thinking is a conscious effort, a work effort in which you not only engage the intellectual center, but also allow the emotional center to participate. One of my daily commitments is, "I want to think from the Work." I feel this will ultimately lead me to the final state: I wish to *live* the Work. This is a different level, where right thinking and right attitudes will govern my life.

Chapter 21

Laziness

At one time I asked each individual in my group, "What shortcomings do you recognize in yourself?" Laziness was mentioned by the majority. One person recognized it as his main feature. It is a factor in all our lives. I wanted to look into what laziness is. Where does it originate? What are its manifestations? What can we do about it?

Laziness is *self-love*. We baby ourselves. We do what we mechanically love to do, what we prefer to do, enjoy doing, and turn away from any effort we would have to make if we turned to the Work.

Laziness is a deep-rooted, common weakness. It appears in all of us. If it is physical it is easy to detect. I don't like to get up from my comfortable chair, sofa or bed. I don't like to go two blocks out of my way to do something that I should do for myself or someone else. I don't want to move faster or do a task which may require physical effort. I may not even want to bend down to pick something up. Whatever I may do, I don't do it as well as it could be done. With each thing I attempt, there are many levels of quality possible in how it is accomplished. How carefully do I make my bed? Do I properly set the table? In my work, laziness is when I see what could be done, what is possible at my level or a little beyond, and *I do not do it*. Combatting laziness is intentional suffering and conscious labor.

There are extremely subtle manifestations of laziness in the intellectual center, and these are harder to see. I do not want to consciously engage my mind. I do not want to read a book which requires attention. I abhor the idea of carefully balancing my checkbook, answering a letter long overdue, even making a business telephone call. When I postpone these things, it can be an alarm clock telling me "Now you are lazy."

Then it goes deeper. Perhaps I have to make a decision involving an emotion, not a vital one, but one that requires considering someone else's needs. Someone may need my reassurance. Another may need me to listen to his or her complaints. If it does not concern me, it may be hard for me to put myself in the other person's place. I am often too lazy to say some comforting words at the right moment or think of what would please the other person. We are too lazy to look into ourselves, to *see* what we ought to do. We are too lazy to listen to our conscience. We each have a conscience and although we may know that conscience exists and *does* help us, it is too much effort to contact it. We may be afraid to hear what it says about the kind of work we must do.

Laziness affects my work. When we were first searching, we had a vague feeling that something wasn't right; we felt that there was a different life possible than the one through which we were drifting. Our magnetic center began slowly developing, helping to focus the direction of our search. Then we encountered the Gurdjieff tradition and we embraced this Work with enthusiasm and vigor. But soon enough it became routine and mechanical. We lost the zest for working and we became truly lost.

Laziness is one of the greatest enemies in our inner work as well as in ordinary life. We must fight it with all the knowledge and understanding the Work has given us. We must observe ourselves, reaffirm the commitment we made to ourselves, and summon energies through the emotional center to make a conscious effort *every time* we see our laziness, whether it is physical, mental or emotional. It requires constant watchfulness, **will** and honesty to go against ourselves.

What is my practical approach and attitude toward laziness? It is establishing a **discipline** in the working of all three centers.

I have to recognize and distinguish which of my centers is involved in each specific case. But I think I have to go further. I have to establish a daily physical discipline and adhere to it—walking, being aware of my breathing, a sport. Mental exercise to combat laziness can be a commitment to read something daily that expands my knowledge, whether in books or in the journal that I have kept of my Work life. I can make it my task to observe in my daily work whether I think consciously or do mental work routinely, mechanically. I can think before I speak. To exercise my lazy emotional center, I can give someone I know a special small gift, a hug, some affection, a smile. I can listen consciously to music, sing, or play an instrument. I can greet someone who has hurt me with kindness and gentleness. The methods to create the energies necessary to combat laziness are described in the chapter on energy.

I see a task and I see my resistance, but I summon the Work and "I try." And then the miracle happens. *Any* effort I make brings in a new and different energy, "energizes" my whole being. The mind becomes stimulated, the lethargy of the body begins to evaporate. I accept the task I have set myself. I make a super-effort beyond my ordinary efforts. I am regenerated, my inner state changes, laziness is defeated by conscious effort. **This is work**.

Chapter 22

Freedom

The wish for freedom comes from a need—as well as a "foretaste"—of freedom and what it could mean to be free. In the state of waking sleep, the sensing of freedom arises from the recognition of its lack. In my sleep at night it is impossible to know freedom, but in waking sleep I can recognize that it is possible to be free, by beginning to see that I am in a prison whose bars and guards are created by me. Therefore, the first question that I can ask is "From what do I wish to be free?"

The foretaste of freedom comes from observations of what it is that keeps me from it. I may recognize, after long work at observing myself, that identification keeps me in my state of sleep. When identified, my outlook, appraisal, valuation of impressions is limited and subjective. If I am identified, nothing new can occur. The image that false personality has created gives strength to identification. I can only begin to be free by seeing and eventually giving up this false image of myself.

I must be "unattached" if the possibility of anything new, of any help, or of any insight is to exist. If there is an opening, a detachment from things (my "possessions," my negativities, or my own particular form of suffering, which feeds my personality), if there can be a separation from my imagination, then the possibility exists of attaining this **state of detachment**. It is from this state that I can begin work at another level. An attachment or identification which takes possession of all of me can serve either a "positive" or a "negative," but precluding any possibility of holding both positive and negative forces at the same time. It is when we can hold both positive and negative at once that there is the possibility of having a third force enter, the neutralizing force.

All of this is very far away. Where do I begin my work on freedom—as I am, in the state that I am in? A machine cannot be free, so I need to be free from mechanicalness. When I am mechanical, I am asleep; there is no possibility of choice in this state. The reverse of this is that in the state of consciousness, *I can choose*. How can this state be achieved? This state begins with an inner quiet, by going into an inner silence, an emptying, a void, so that an inner listening can occur. In this state of quiet an attention may manifest itself which could connect me with a higher consciousness. If my "outside" mind is made to function in its proper place and not take possession of *all* of me, if this mind can be put "in neutral," not reverting to yesterday nor anticipating tomorrow, then something can take place in this present moment. But this is still much too far from my present state. Let me give some examples of what is meant by freedom and prison.

I knew a professor of mathematics with a beautifully organized intellect who lived as if all of life could be "solved" by his mind. Can transformation be possible for a person in this state? Can such a person receive any new thoughts or be free from identification? He asked me the question, "What is freedom? How can I separate myself from my way of thinking, which is intellectual and does not allow me, enable me to *feel*?" He was beginning to recognize how habitually his mind functions and how it is a barrier to the expression of emotions toward his wife, children, even his students. He began to realize that, by freeing himself from his mind, it could create a new, different life.

Another person in my group reacts whenever change of mind or transformation is brought up and responds, "Well, that's me; I can't help it!" However, she *could* help it if she realized how chained she is to uncritical acceptance of herself as she is now. Freeing herself from her ever-recurring attitude and recognizing her mechanical acceptance ("that's me") would give her the incentive for making efforts to get out of her prison.

There was a poet who was a wonderful word-smith but was

unable and unwilling to *think*. Almost everything flowed out of him. Freeing himself from his imagination, running wild to the point of almost drowning him, he could change and save his life.

We may achieve freedom in moments of consciousness if we would use the power of "the wish" and practice it for years. Recognizing our own self-deceit, we are able to see our entrapments, our own particular prison. Another person I know saw that he was going in circles instead of upward spirals. He could see how he made the same mistakes in life, again and again. This person made freedom his aim, his God.

Sometimes we can see how frequently we fall into the deep abyss of negative states and recognize the necessity of being free of this disease in order to live a useful and satisfying life. This recognition is a step toward freedom.

I asked, on one occasion, "From what do you wish to be free?" Here are some responses:

Freedom from my outer self;

Freedom from habitual (mechanical) thoughts;

Freedom from confusion;

Freedom from fear;

Freedom from something that prevents me from achieving a change;

Freedom from self-deceit;

Freedom from thinking in circles;

Freedom from imagination, wild and negative emotional thoughts;

Freedom from my main feature provided I know what it is;

Freedom

Freedom to *feel*;

Freedom to express myself;

Freedom to see myself and to be honest with myself;

Freedom to find the door which allows me to enter a new world in which I am free;

Freedom from mechanical life, from mechanicalness, from waking sleep.

Chapter 23

The Sitting

The following experiences come directly from my work diaries. I relate them to show my own struggles in this very personal work on myself, *not* as a model or guide. It is important for each individual to allow herself or himself to have his or her own unique experience.

March 3, 1986

In the exercise in the morning, I have a distinct sensation that the end of the sitting is near. I sense my legs, a distinct dark grey fog surrounds me, a void, an emptiness. I feel it around my forehead, my eyes. I feel I am in a different dimension, I am somewhere else than the person that started the sitting. The timer rings; forty minutes are over. I know it is possible to preserve this sensation, prolong the sitting, but do I? No, I get up from my sitting cushion, a zafu, and stop with regrets at seeing my weakness.

March 13, 1986

The deepest exercise. No thoughts, no interference. It felt very long, an existence in a different world. No sensation of the physical body, but at the same time a clear sensing of the body. Best quality I've ever had. No wish interfered. For a fleeting moment, something drifted through my mind, "Maybe enlightenment can come." No need for a life after. I have the realization that this is the life I have been given and this is the life I have the right to experience every waking moment. Should I get up and write it down or should I continue, not breaking the mood? This is a frequent dilemma for me. I remained in the place where I was.

The Sitting

November 15, 1986

I had the worst sitting in years. I was nervous, lacked energy, direction, attention and will. I almost approached negativity, but controlled the latter through self-observation. I finally stopped this sitting. I am glad that I have the courage to admit this here.

November 21, 1986

It took about thirty minutes of struggle before sinking into nothingness. I tried to empty my mind but saw the thoughts creeping in unhindered. I catch them, blank out for maybe three or four minutes, and another chain of thoughts returns, many of them connected with the difficulties of the coming day, all imagined because none of them materialized.

• • • •

As I begin my sitting I have no wish; I am just aware of myself. I sense myself, I relax and try to be totally present, without any thought. Then a new state forms itself in me. I have the feeling "I am taking an inner shower," from the head all the way down to my toes. It washes away all the obstructions to a deeper understanding, the obstacles which hinder higher cosmic forces from entering and filling me.

• • • •

I have to start with the commitment to total immobility when I begin my sitting. The back has to be absolutely straight, because it keeps the mind alert. A slouching posture, a bent back, will make the mind lazy. To get the fullest benefit and value out of a sitting, the emotional center has to be active, because it creates finer vibrations.

• • • •

Sitting may begin like boarding an airplane on a drizzly, foggy morning. The plane takes off and there is gray all around.

All of a sudden it breaks through the fog and you are above the sea of clouds, under a blue sky in bright sunshine.

• • • •

March 22, 1987

I woke up about 12:30 at night, got up, then returned again to bed for about 10 minutes. My *body*, more than the mind, was wide awake, although I longed to sleep, to feel the pleasant lethargy of sleep. My "life conscience" was telling me, "I have to get up early and I won't have time to sit in the morning." But it was my body that forced me out of bed and into the usual place for the morning exercise in my den. The body was quiet at once. The mind was empty. There was no wish, no aim, no compulsion, nothing forced or asked for; this emptiness "just happened."

I was breathing rather slowly, sometimes deep, sometimes shallow. I lost myself in the "void." It was a friendly void, not at all alien. It was as if I were part of it and belonged. There was nothing I had to "do," nothing I had to strive for. It was natural, as death is natural. For a long time prior to this, I have felt that it was necessary to attempt to exclude all thoughts in my sittings. I came to understand that this is only the first step. Upon arriving at the void, the emptiness, the unknown, you must **allow something to happen**. Then new thoughts, impressions and expressions can arise. Entering the void may be frightening but it does not have to be so. It can be light and free. This was what I felt in this sitting. It was acceptance mixed with promise and hope.

After forty minutes, I went back to bed. Sleep came, and then morning, and with it realizations in the form of a warm light. Now I understood the word "**being**" with my innermost essence. I *knew* what **being** is. I had always heard the word in the phrase "I wish to be." Now the true meaning of it had reality for me. In other sittings, I have felt myself drifting upward like a cloud, like a whitish smoke rising from a campfire in the open. At other times I have had to struggle.

• • • •

As you begin your sitting, follow the obligatory routine. Go around the body three times in the prescribed manner, observing the mind and at the same time quieting thoughts, body, emotions. At times it doesn't get off the ground. You are heavy. You are anchored in life, something doesn't allow you to let go. If this occurs, revert to conscious efforts.

When the sitting is especially difficult for you, it is possible to focus your attention on breathing. It must come naturally. You may see that it is either shallow or very deep. Do not interfere with it, but only observe.

At other times, being quiet and relaxed comes easily, naturally, so naturally that even the wish "to be quiet" is disturbing and lessens the effect. This is the most desirable state. We can achieve it, but we must be sensitive to our inner receiving apparatus to catch the exact moment to enter infinity.

These are the directives: "As you sit down, make this *commitment* to yourself: 'I wish to sit as quietly as I possibly can.'" You must sit every day, preferably at the same time and in the same place—a place which is saturated with the vibrations of hundreds of previous sittings. But sitting is only the beginning of your daily work. You have to consecrate some of the day to inner work every day, not only for the sitting.

I have questioned myself about why total immobility is required in our morning sittings and what this immobility produces. There is a process going on in me that is so fine that even a thought can disturb it, since thought is material—and very coarse material. It can be compared to a cobweb, which is destroyed by the slightest touch or movement, or to a soap bubble—existing, visible, but dissolving into nothingness when touched.

I don't really know the answer, but I sense the absolute necessity of producing this quietness as my own contribution to
transformation from the coarser into the finer. This immobility
has its own vibrations, starting deep inside of me and slowly
spreading outward. When I achieve it, a transformation is in
process.

At times, I start my sitting with visualization. You visualize
the utmost quiet state possible. Visualization is the language of
the emotional center. It is the reins between the coachman and
the horse. The emotional center *can* make contact with the
higher emotional center, the source of help. The emotional center has to be involved to get the best quality in your sitting. It
has the finest vibrations.

I try to see myself as a whole in my sittings (and at other
times as well), not only as parts of myself. This means that I try
to see simultaneously my thoughts, my emotions, my sensations, moods, movements, postures, tone of voice if I am speaking, facial expressions, to get the full picture of myself.
Hitherto I may have had more partial snapshots of certain habitual movements, certain facial expressions characteristic of a
particular mood. But it is the entire picture which allows me to
see what part of myself needs attention at the moment, on what
part I have to begin my work.

• • • •

November 8, 1987

I got up in the very early morning for my usual sitting, the
best time of the day for me. As I sat down, I made a commitment for total inner immobility. This time, however, it must
have come from a different place. There was not a muscle
which moved, no thought coming from the intellectual center
which interfered, but there were thoughts coming from somewhere.

I felt something take place NOW.

I felt what transformation could be NOW.

I sensed there is another world NOW.

It was physical, in a very subtle way, but undeniable. It led to the sensation—or should I say belief, or conviction?—that a second Being Body can exist and is formed in this immobility. I could and did fully understand that this body is on a different plane and operates under different laws, having access to higher, finer energies, which—if we are open to them—can influence our entire being, the being that can be the making of our life.

I wanted to go on sitting and sitting, way beyond the customary 40 minutes. This was the quality I always was striving for but rarely achieved. Normally, it was always "in" my mind or recognized by the mind. This time it was in all of me.

"I wish to crystallize my second Being Body, to live under its laws which come from a different world."

December 20, 1988

It was 2:30 A.M. in my den. As I sat down, I was in a dark void. I was free of the sensation of my entire body. It did not exist. But something or someone was there and alive. I truly felt it was a higher body, something I have been working on for years and an aim which is necessary for me to achieve.

A pain in my right leg arose at one point in the sitting. Normally, with this particular pain, I stretch the leg to relieve the pain. This time the thought entered, "I am master of myself; I will not give in." Miraculously, the pain subsided. This was the only thought which entered in the entire sitting. My mind, an adversary of many a sitting, was blank and was completely free of my body. At the beginning, I was aware of entering a blackness, a cosmic blackness, a different world, but even this disappeared.

Forty-five minutes passed. I could have stayed longer, I was in a timeless space, but the usual conflict arose. What is better for me, to continue or to stop and savor this experience while I am still filled with it? Or should I write down this exceptional experience in my journal for the benefit of sharing it with my students? I continued sitting.

This night the mood of some preceding days had completely changed. Laziness, lack of energy, even the interest in inner work which had filled me, was dispelled. A great calmness permeated all of me. I was as aware of death as I was of the room in which I sat—the couch, the chair, the rugs. There was no emotion or thought involved, just an awareness, nothing else.

Guides for Inner Work

These are examples of directions for inner work which I occasionally distribute to members of my groups at our meetings to ponder during the week, called "Work Guides."

I wish to be.

What does this mean?

I don't know, I do not want to verbalize it, but I feel the **wish**.

What can I do about it?

I make a solemn commitment to be **quiet, quiet**.

I sense my limbs,

I sense my body,

I am aware of my mind, my empty mind.

I have to practice this every day, **allow something to happen**.
Then one day I will get the taste of *being*.

• • • •

My wish must come from a deep, deep *need*.

It must come from my entire being and from every part of me.

All my centers must be involved, my body must participate,

must sense it, recognize this need.

I must be aware of my nothingness,

I must be at the end of my rope;

it must be a question of life and death.

Only then may I expect my wish to be heard,

to be fulfilled, and then not in my time, but in **God's** time.

• • • •

We cannot change a situation in life.

What we can do and have to do is

to change our **attitude** toward the situation.

• • • •

If you fear the truth, you will always *give way to the voices of resistance*, and not even hear the struggling cry of something deep within that is being starved and therefore cannot grow.

You need great **courage** in this work.

• • • •

I ask you today, "What help do you want from the work?"

I want to expand my knowledge . . .

I want to expand my being, my understanding . . .

I want to achieve inner freedom . . .

I want to **discipline** myself . . .

Above all, I want to be **Master of myself**.

• • • •

Try not to pursue a thought
entering your mind by **thinking**,
unless it is *useful*.

• • • •

Tomorrow will be the product
of what I am today.

• • • •

Real prayer is a cosmic substance
if properly produced.

• • • •

If you express negative emotions you are in their power.
At that moment you can do nothing.
The stopping of expressions of negative emotions
and the struggle with negative emotions
are two different practices.
This has to be understood.

• • • •

A Spiritual Accounting

Five questions to ask oneself before retiring:

1. What did I do well today?

2. What did I do today that I should not have done?

3. What didn't I do today that I should have done?

4. What did I do that I could have done better?

5. What do I want to do tomorrow?

• • • •

"The ideas are a summons, a summons towards another world, a call from one who knows and is able to show us the way. But the transformation of the human being requires something more. It can only be achieved if there is a real meeting between the conscious force which descends and the total commitment that answers it. This brings about a fusion.

"A new life can then appear in a new set of conditions, which only someone with an objective consciousness can create and develop."

From Jeanne de Salzmann's foreword to *Views From the Real World*

• • • •

Why am I sitting "**quiet**"?

Because this way all my energy is contained within me.

I do not leak energy now.

• • • •

The morning exercise is your bridge to the unknown,

the void.

You must build this bridge

and then cross it.

• • • •

This quiet has its own vibrations.
In doing our sittings we try to put our body
into the same quiet, and little by little we achieve
the same high vibrations through our entire organism.
The quiet allows a transformation of the coarser into the finer.

• • • •

Make a place inside you to be able to hear.
All our lives depend on the way we listen internally.

• • • •

You have to consecrate
some time of the day,
each day,
to your inner work.

• • • •

Only when thoughts are stopped
can thinking begin.

• • • •

The **state** of your morning exercise
and the state afterwards in life are different.
Observe this in you,
Become aware of breathing, and
you may bring them together.

• • • •

When I sit quietly in the morning
I perform inner disengagement.

• • • •

I sit here. I see myself. But what do I see? I see the image I have of myself, not who I really am, not who I really wish to be.

So, what is my aim? It is to reach a higher level of development, to make contact with my higher centers, and through them establish a contact with "the inner circle of humanity," with cosmic forces which are always surrounding us ready to help us in our inner and outer work.

Who can do this? A different I, not the false image I have of myself. I have to destroy this image now. I have to build not on sand but on rock, to become a different person. This is a very painful process.

It is voluntary suffering and friction which helps us to grow, which helps the inner transformation for which we are in the Work. I want to leave you with these thoughts, these tools. Only you can apply them.

97

And so I end this with a prayer:

Lord, help me to lead a life

which warrants my existence.